ONE-TWO

by Igor Eliseev

Glagoslav Publications

ONE–TWO

by Igor Eliseev

Edited by Jonathan Finch

Publishers Maxim Hodak & Max Mendor

© 2015, Igor Eliseev
Cover illustrations © 2015, Igor Eliseev

© 2016, Glagoslav Publications, United Kingdom

Glagoslav Publications Ltd
88-90 Hatton Garden
EC1N 8PN London
United Kingdom

www.glagoslav.com

ISBN: 978-1-911414-23-0

A catalogue record for this book
is available from the British Library.

ONE-TWO

by Igor Eliseev

𝓬

Igor Eliseev

To my mother

The Tawpies

My God, it's so cold. You look happy while asleep and I can't stop thinking about how cold I am. Why is it so chilly here? I just can't get warm, the same as in the hospital when they plunged us into ice water. We tried our best to get out of the bathtub clinging to the edge but Ivan Borisovich told us to calm down and keep quiet. Do you remember him? His office door was furnished by a wooden sign plate designating his high position, that's why we were forced to do everything he told us to. The water was freezing and seemed to pierce our bodies with thousands of needles; I couldn't breathe and couldn't get used to it. I can hardly remember how long it lasted but have always dreamt of forgetting about it. Unfortunately, a short time later, you fell severely ill, and Ivan Borisovich put us into the isolation cell. Lying there, you would often abruptly get up on our bed and breathe heavily and insatiably, swallowing the air. Sometimes your chest made gurgling sounds; you spat out sputum and lay down again. I was lying next to you threatened by the thought that you could die. In a couple of days, I got ill too.

The isolation cell represented a small room with a tiny gridded window, an old squeaky bed near the wall and a wash-stand to the left, a mirror and a toilet-bowl to the right. A tightly locked door was accompanied by a little stool. Auntie Masha, a bow-backed, broad-hipped woman always wearing her white cap, brought us food. Ivan Borisovich called her a custodian. Our meals included two large mugs of weak tea or hot water. I sipped half of my portion and soaked an edge of our sheet in the other half and applied the sheet to my chest and then to yours. Shortly before the New Year there was a thaw and the snow outside melted almost completely. Our room was lit by bright sunlight through the window grids and shiny knives of light pointed to the part where our bodies were joined.

When we felt a little better, auntie Masha brought two oranges under her white robe and handed them to us and wished us good health. You ate your orange unpeeled right under your blanket and I gave you mine hoping it would help you to get well sooner. Now I understand the absurdity of that act because *we are a whole*. I am you and you are me.

I can hardly tell a thing about our childhood. Too bad that you are sleeping now; I wish you could help me recall something from the past. The New Year's thaw and oranges are my brightest memories. I also remember you playing as if you were my mom and caressing my head but you never let me do that to you, pushed my hand away and grumbled. The only time you let our mother touch you happened much later.

Another thing I remember was bedtime stories. Auntie Masha, always short of breath, whispering and glancing at the door from time to time, read us fairy-tales about faraway places, blue seas and charming princes who were supposed to appear before us and take both of us away to some beautiful land. Back then, I believed it was possible. I think that is the reason why all grown-ups reminisce about their childhood with such a melancholic look in their eyes. I knew the Ugly Duckling story almost by heart; the final part where he turns into a beautiful swan was my favorite. I used to imagine ourselves experiencing that kind of transformation, immersed in an imaginary reality. Apparently, I felt the need to change but didn't know yet what to do. That was before we saw ourselves in the mirror.

* * *

A difficult delivery took place in one of the maternity homes in the capital city. Twins were born, one of them being larger in size and the other feeble and low weight. A lot of doctors gathered in a room number nine to take a look at this unprecedented miracle. Windows of the room overlooked an adorable orchard; I'm sure it is even more beautiful these days. A midwife fainted at the sight of two conjoined babies and another doctor had to extract us. Initially, the maternity-home staff planned to tell our mother we had died but after a while one of the nurses on duty showed us to her. Our mother had a fit, and soon after her mental health degenerated. Persuaded by the hospital management, she signed a certificate of our death. Our father was away on business at the time and received the news of our decease by an ordinary telegram.

Later on, the doctors often told us frightening stories about life-threatening pregnancy complications accompanied by bleeding which could have been fatal to our mother and the Herculean efforts she had made to bring us into the world whole and undamaged. It seemed like she was a Hero of Labor.

For several years we have been experimental subjects, first at the institute of pediatrics and then at the institute of traumatology where the above-mentioned Ivan Borisovich studied us. It is now impossible to find out who gave us names. It certainly wasn't our parents because they haven't been in our life since its very beginning. Our birth certificate states: Nadezhda (*left*), Vera (*right*)[1]; somebody was probably afraid to make a mistake. I am Faith and together we are called conjoined

---

1   The meanings of Russian names *Vera* and *Nadezhda* are "faith" and "hope" respectively. Hereinafter the names *Faith* and *Hope* will be used.

twins. Such a thing does exist in nature and it happens to be us. We look very much alike but have different personalities, just like ordinary people.

Seemingly, when Ivan Borisovich had enough of his scientific activity we were transferred to a closed boarding school to receive our elementary education. I associate the best years of our life with that place. There were no grids on the windows and we could feel like normal children for the first time in our life. Every morning we were woken up by the birds living in handmade nesting boxes outside. From the window we could see a nearby forest and smell pine wood and moss in the windy air rushing in through the open vent pane. That's where we met Lizzie.

Her real name was Evangeline but for some reason she preferred being called Lizzie. She looked very young, sixteen at most, but actually she turned out to be twenty-two, which came to our knowledge by chance. You could guess her age only by observing the extremely deep creases between her eyebrows, visible on her face even when she was calm. It is hard to describe her in a couple of words. For me, Lizzie was an embodiment of fireworks bursting with thousands of emotional colors and shades never seen in one person before. She granted a sense of endless festivity, combining a genuinely childish nature with the experience of a wise woman. She would sometimes play little pranks disturbing all the boarding school staff but after a minute would sit in a corner staring at the floor. Lizzie seemed to know everything about people; I wonder who taught her all those things. She used to speak only positively even of people who hurt her willingly or unwillingly. Since that time we have never met with such an open-hearted and trusting person, though she did hide certain things — her early pregnancy, for instance. We learned about it only after a few weeks. Her parents made her have an abortion when they learnt the truth (it had happened during the 1980 Olympics[2]). Lizzie's mind became disturbed and they sent her to the boarding school for rehabilitation. Truly speaking, they rather wished to hide their disgraceful daughter from society than help her. Her parents were "great guns" in the Party[3], Lizzie's words, and they considered her accidental pregnancy by a black Cuban athlete to be an unforgivable mistake.

Once upon a time she wandered into our room by chance, sat on the floor and scrutinized us for a long time very carefully and unabashedly. Then she took a sheet of paper, put it on the chair standing nearby and got down to drawing. We were sitting on our bed, afraid to make a movement, not understanding what was going on and absolutely at a loss for what to say. After finishing her work, Lizzie glanced at us with such genuine surprise as if she had just found out we were there. "Hi. I'm Lizzie. Would you like me to do more drawings of you?" after which she left us, not even waiting for an answer.

We were intrigued by this extraordinary episode and for several days thereafter we looked out for a chance to meet her again, anywhere, but we had no luck. However, after a week precisely, she sneaked into our room through the open window and appeared before us herself. Our door was never locked but Lizzie said she found window-climbing much easier and more exciting. She acted open-heartedly, at ease, as if she had known us forever. Sitting on a spare bed,

---

2 1980 Summer Olympics, officially known as the Games of the XXII Olympiad, were held in Moscow, Soviet Union, in present day Russia, from July 19 to August 3, 1980.

3 Refers to the governing party of the USSR, the Communist Party, at that time one of the largest left-wing radical organizations in the world.

Lizzie took out her sketchbooks and notebooks and started demonstrating her skill in drawing. At first she was silent and simply handed us her papers like a child playing with its speechless reflection, then she went on to explain. "Look, it's so clear that the two of you, on some level, belong together, as lovers, or as friends, but in this picture, there's me standing between you. What happens to other people will happen to you." Her collection contained a surprisingly large number of pictures of conjoined girls although she was fond of drawing many different people: house-parents, passersby, doctors. One of the drawings showed you being nearly twice as tall and big as me, another represented a portrait of us having colored faces; mine was pink and yours was blue. In some pictures we were portrayed uglier than we actually were: I had a ludicrous beard and moustache and you demonstrated a beaming smile on your square face; we were crossing and stretching, thickening and expanding. She stuck our backs together in such a way that we would never be able to see each other, or joined our shoulders weirdly leaving me only with the left arm and you only with the right. In fact, each of us has two arms and two legs and we are conjoined at the hip, but Lizzie saw us in her own way and depicted us totally different from reality. I really liked that picture where we were picking flowers in pretty dresses; we had large, beautiful eyes and our hair was down, touching the ground. But the last picture, to me, was very embarrassing: without turning an eyelash, Lizzie portrayed us naked, with our breasts, which we haven't got, legs and bellies, and our entire bodies totally exposed. You, on the contrary, were delighted with the drawing; I remember you studying it for a long while, after which you asked, "Could you draw us separately?" Lizzie burst out laughing, then took a cigarette and lit it. "Silly, young girls, you don't understand a thing. The point is that you are not like everyone else; you're the real *tawpies*. Just think how great it is to be you!"

I remember she confessed to us one day, "Staying here is more than any artist could dream of. You can lead a rackety life to your heart's content, as long as it doesn't confuse people around you. Actually, even if they do get confused, what's so bad about that?" Then we asked her why she chose to involve herself in drawing. "Why do I draw? What do you mean why?" she repeated trying to sense the taste of the words. "This is how I respond to reality. Words are insufficient to express all my feelings. Few adults whose thoughts and acts are always perfectly correct listen to me unless I wear a *white robe*. Convinced of their ultimate rightness, they never get tired of hurting me, keeping up appearances. They never get the point: it doesn't matter whether you are right or wrong; the only thing that matters is whether people around you are happy about your way of doing things. My images might be unreal, not corresponding to forms, contours, colors, and through them I obviously "lie" to people, but they are the only truth for me. I only wish my parents, who are supposed to be the dearest people on earth to me, could understand me. They are the only ones I wouldn't be able to portray, not because I bear a grudge against them, but because I am not interested in them. Their life is similar to the eternal late fall when all the shades have faded away and become gray. From people, they turned into living codes of rules, laws and prejudices — lifeless shadows in an ordinary dining room where they seem to be quite happy with served food and drinks. So why do I draw? Personally to me, it gives me the possibility of feeling the world and people, of perceiving their pain and pleasure, of admiring the surrounding beauty; my drawings are confessions of my love for the world."

I believed, sooner or later, adults would listen to her words if only Lizzie didn't get drunk so often. She spent the allowance from her parents on alcohol, which was delivered right to her room. Let's say, she never suffered a shortage of booze. All the medical personnel pretended to be unaware of this, but, to hand it to Lizzie, she was really good at drinking. She could fuddle all night long and wake up fresh as a daisy the next morning. But there were days when her spirits were terribly down; she often burst into tears and behaved completely intolerably. On those days she swallowed handfuls of pills and washed them down with alcohol trying to hide her frustration and anxiety, to escape from reality for evermore. At times she seemed to hear a baby crying somewhere; she intermittently ran up to the window and to the door and then came back to her place again. First we attentively listened to all indistinct sounds trying to discern something, but in vain; our hearts always used to leap when she had such seizures. By the way, it was Lizzie who introduced us to alcohol. The first time we tasted "the Gift of the Magi", as she called it, was a few weeks after we met her. I remember that after the first glass we got really dizzy, fell on to a bed and were unable to get up for a long time; Lizzie teased us and couldn't stop laughing loudly, then got tired and proceeded to do some drawing. We were tossing on a bed with our feet trailing on the floor; all that resembled some sort of drunken madness. Hardly had we sat up on our bed, still groggy, with blurred eyes, when she jumped up right next to us and asked, "Do you happen to know that many people take kissing in public as a personal insult?" I doubt she cared the slightest about what we thought. "Believe it or not, guys hate it when girls slobber in their mouths; they prefer experienced women. However, I think I can teach you a good lesson."

So she did. Firmly squeezing her mouth up against our lips and almost chewing them off, she kept repeating incessantly, "Like this, got it? There you go!" But when we became a little better at it, she suddenly jerked back and shouted, "Whatever do you think you're doing? Have you gone bonkers?"

We were stupefied. We stared at her.

Meanwhile, Lizzie went up to a window, sat on the sill, lowered her feet down and uttered, staring somewhere into the woods, "This whole world is a huge mental home where miserable people are all involved in a contest to make the greatest nonsense or go mad first." Then she turned to us and added, "My congratulations, you would win a prize, no doubt about it!" After that her face acquired a wistful and melancholic expression, except for her bold eyes; a little later she started running back and forth and shouting gibberish. I tried to help and grabbed her by the hand, but Lizzie got very frightened, stared at me, and yelled desperately, "Leave me alone! You don't understand anything, silly girls! It is all meaningless! What's the use of looking for anything, what's the use of trusting, loving, if all of us are going to decay in a wooden box anyway?!" Nurses heard the sounds of her yelling, came running and tried to tie her up and tranquilize her, but Lizzie resisted and kicked her feet like a wild mare when they grasped her by the hands. The impression was that her strength would suffice for ten people. Only after a good few doctors had gathered in our room did they manage to pacify her by giving her a sedative shot. A minute later she went limp and fell asleep. Right afterwards, we found her drawing on our bed, distorted stuff, as if you were looking at the world from under water.

After that incident we didn't see each other for a long time. Lizzie stayed in another building and received special treatment. We mostly languished alone in our room. And when we finally met again she didn't even mention the last drawing of her series and we were so eager to keep it that we didn't say a word, either. We could never understand why she cried that day.

One day when we were having dinner in the dining room, Lizzie came up to us and said, "You know what? I envy you! You will never be lonely, which sooner or later happens to everyone, but not to you." I asked her why people are lonely and she answered, "People are selfish. Most of them only pretend to love someone while in fact the only people they love are themselves. Instead of confessing their love, they ask: do you love me? And all those lofty feelings they proclaim they believe in are a mere romantic flight of the imagination; in truth, they simply want someone always beside them. By all means they try to gain sole ownership of someone but are not capable of committing themselves in return; then comes everyday routine followed by boredom; the illusory love dies, giving place to alienation that foredooms people to even greater loneliness. Love not only means unification and preservation, but it is also the process of creation, too; people know about this, but somehow never remember." In retrospect, our time with Lizzie really taught us a lot, more than all the time without her. Our worthless life meant something when we were with her and she was talking to us.

However, other dwellers of the boarding school saw us the way we actually were and the way we saw ourselves for the first time many years ago. Before we hadn't had the chance to face large mirrors; doctors at the institute of traumatology used only small, portable ones. I can clearly remember the day when Ivan Borisovich put a cabinet-sized mirror in his office and stood by it. It had lighting on its edges. They brought us in front of it and left us alone. We had seen ourselves before, in reflections in windows and on glass doors attached to medical cabinets, but that time was the most painful. All the doctors standing in the hall were looking at us very attentively. Dispassionately, Ivan Borisovich wrote something with enthusiasm. You started smiling and gesticulating intensely but all I wanted to do was to run away that very minute; suddenly I realized why everybody stared at us. I literally lost my firm ground, my head started spinning; having lost my balance for a second, I tumbled down on to the floor and dragged you with me. I remember that I hurt myself badly and tears started streaming down my face. The floor was terribly cold and you attempted to get up at once, but I just wanted to lie down and cry. I couldn't protest and shout because I had no strength left; instead I lay there and refused to get back to my feet. "An interesting case," Ivan Borisovich remarked; "I would call this behavior motor adynamia." From then on, this term has been used to explain every disagreement between you and me. Finally, someone helped us to get up and brought us back to our room. But now I knew for sure: my true mirror was you. You have always understood and accepted my most genuine, most intimate impulses and responded to them with surprising accuracy. I wish all people turned into such mirrors for each other.

It is hard to tell at what age I started to have dreams in which I was alone. Of course, it was like I knew that you were always around, but, nevertheless, we were each by herself, separated from each other. In my dreams, my own world expressed itself fully and became visible, absolutely visible. I was confidently running along the corridor, flying and falling, or finding myself in a mysterious castle full of obscurities and secrets. The sense of freedom I had gained was filling me with lightness and comfort even when I could not feel my feet anymore; at that moment I usually stumbled and fell into emptiness. After waking up I found you peacefully sleeping to the right of me, as always, the way I see you now.

I cannot remember all the details of that rainy August morning. We were sitting in our room and I was reading aloud the story of a tiny, little boy with golden hair[4] who was looking for a lamb. Once upon a time a pilot arrived in a white plane and did him a drawing of a lamb in a box, a muzzle for the lamb so that it couldn't eat the boy's flower, and even a leash to keep it from running away. But one day a snake bit the child and he died. His death was supposed to send him back to where he came from; as people go back to the earth, the kid with golden hair went back to the stars.

You and I were speculating on the fairy tale we had just read and suddenly heard an unusual fuss in the corridors of the boarding house, people's hubbub and hasty shuffling sounds. We put the book aside and left the room following the sounds like rats charmed by a magic flute. Unfortunately, we couldn't find out what had happened. One of the doctors yelled at us and ordered us back into our room, so we dragged back. Soon, from our window we saw an ambulance and people in white robes carrying a litter; something was definitely going on. Later we peeped into the dining room to ask the cooks about the incident, but they kept their silence as if their lives depended on it, so we had nothing to do but to return to our room again. We were not in the mood to continue discussing the book and were just looking out of the window without a word. Little by little, a strange, unpleasant premonition seized us. I felt that something irreparable had happened and things would never be the same from that moment on. And it was true. That rainy morning our poor Lizzie had jumped out of the window.

---

4   Novella by Antoine de Saint-Exupéry, *The Little Prince*.

Lizzie was overly vulnerable, excessively fragile and way too special to have a good chance of living long. She had the same golden bush of hair as that kid from the book, and her *flight* from a window turned out to be her bright retrieval of the stars. Obviously, we are those ugly ducklings everyone leaves. We cried all night long, and in the morning you told me, "Faith, promise me you will never cry again with Hope." I think you matured dramatically that night and became the one I could rely on.

One day Lizzie saw us going down the stairs. We try to perform this operation, simple for ordinary people, slowly and in unison. Coordinating our movements and supporting each other, we take turns, lowering our legs cautiously, first the left pair of legs, then the right. At the sight of this scene Lizzie's dreamily wide-open, permanently astonished, blue eyes became even larger.

"Gosh and hell!" she exclaimed. "It never fails to amaze me how often life generously grants people opportunities and talents, which they neglect for the sake of comfortable, sated and completely mediocre lives which they don't appreciate in the slightest. Some of them are given everything other people would dream of; so probably they should do nothing else but take advantage of their talents and exercise them, but they don't. Their lives are limited by comfort, idle laziness and full stomachs. You are totally different. You are having a hard time doing even the simplest of things. If you could gain the abilities of ordinary people — who knows, perhaps, you would even learn to fly. People must be grateful for your existence! I am."

After the incident, the parents of the deceased girl made a terrible fuss in the boarding school. The higher authorities became seriously disturbed that the school accommodates people with various forms of diseases which result in additional threats to the health of vulnerable groups, some of them ending up in mortuaries. Because doctors *determined* that Lizzie had dropped out of a window accidentally when she slipped on a wet ledge, a few of the doctors were dismissed and most of the patients were sent to other boarding schools. As for us, we were supposed to be transferred to a foster home for children with movement disorders.

Unfortunately, I don't know what happened to Lizzie's drawings. They might have been burnt or handed over to her parents, or maybe they are still resting in that shrivelled bedside table by her bed. We kept the only one she forgot in our room; in the top right corner of it there is an inscription: "The Tawpies". I guess Lizzie didn't even manage to finish it, like all the other deeds in her life, but we thought it was the most beautiful thing we had ever seen. In effect, everything she did was beautiful and amazing... However, if you wish to live a long and peaceful life, you *shouldn't* be like Lizzie.

Order Numbers

A low minibus with a red cross on the door was waiting for us at the exit. A youngish woman with a ponderous face, an employee of the boarding school, accompanied us to the car. The sun rolled up over the horizon, foretelling a nice clear day, and swallows twittered their good-byes to us. A tall, middle-aged man with an inexpressive face was hanging about near the car. He was wearing trousers soiled with fuel oil and a leather jacket, although it was a warm September day. At the sight of us he gave a whistle and drew himself up to his full height. Very impressive he was.

"Blimey!" he exclaimed. "I saw all kinds of stuff here, but this is really something," and spat on the ground amply, accidentally smearing his sleeve.

The employee accompanying us rapidly handed him some papers and a satchel with our belongings and uttered:

"You are going to have a really jolly trip. I personally could never get used to these two," and she nodded towards us. "They are not so bad because they're striplings, but when they grow up they will turn into haggish toads. So what time do you finish today?"

"First I'm gonna deliver 'em to the address and then drop in to the repair shop; the suspension is kinda giving me pain again."

"Well, should I wait for you today or not?" the broad-faced woman insisted.

"I guess you should," he said uncertainly. "If I've got time, I'll pick you up at seven and then we're off to my place. So get prepared for a feat of arms, Stakhanovite[5]."

We stood nearby, literally a stone's throw away from them, with a strange feeling that we were ghosts — neglected, abandoned, lost. At last the tall fellow in a shabby jacket gave a firm hug to his "army wife" with both his hands and, grabbing the curvy bottom of her back, finally dropped with significance:

"Well, wait, wait, maybe."

The broad-faced woman gave us a last look and weakly waved, barely containing her disgust.

The fellow helped us to get into the back seat of the minibus, took the driver's seat, and we hastily shot off, rushed outside the fencing as if we were running away from invisible pursuers.

For a while we rode in silence; we were afraid he was embarrassed, and he probably felt the same as us. However, he must have been suffering from the silence that had emerged, so he started asking us the kinds of questions that we were used to being asked. He took interest in virtually everything: where we were born, what we did in the boarding school, if we had gone to school before that, if we could swim and dance. But one thing that was bothering him the most was whether both of us or only one of us presumably had to obtain a driver's license and how we would be able to drive if we got a license? "Who decides which one of you is going to push the throttle pedal and which one's to pull the brake?" he

---

5   Stakhanovite - a worker of the socialism era achieving the highest labor productivity, the most effective use of equipment and overachievement of production plans in a Soviet-style workplace competition by overcoming of old technical norms and the existing design capacities.

exclaimed, shuddering with horror, but received no answer, after which he laughed kindly for no reason and changed the subject.

What a surprise it was for us to find out that our "lengthy" driver took more interest in science books than in his Stakhanovite. But it is what it is; people are inquisitive creatures. Hurrying to show his knowledge, he started talking hastily and disconnectedly about the fact that time is essentially relative, and passes with a different speed for different people; however, this difference is insignificant and therefore not so obvious. But there are *exceptions*. He scratched the back of his head thoughtfully and added: "I mean, my sister's two years older than me but looks about ten years younger. So she gets older much more slowly than me. Dat is one heck of a thing, and you're telling me 't can't be true." Actually we hadn't said a word, but he was listening only to himself. Having blown his nose loudly on a sleeve of his jacket, he continued with excitement: "An' let's say if one of you suddenly started growin' old much more swiftly than the other one, well, some twenty years later you wouldn't be looking so much alike. An' people watchin' you would think dat one of you is a mother and the other one's a daughter," he concluded yawning expressively. I tried to imagine that, but the very thought of it made me shiver. Living with insuperable, individual differences would be a real nightmare to me. It only makes sense when we grow together and gain experience at the same time. But the big fellow quickly comforted us, "Don't you worry, nothing of dat kind will probably happen to you. Not for everyone time's speedin' up dat much as for me. Actually, it's a very big rarity. Besides, you have already had really tough luck, and lightning never strikes twice in the same place." He spat again and smiled showing black and yellow teeth.

A really weird man, I have to admit, but I still liked him. All the way to the foster-home he was smiling, joking, trying to teach us how to drive, patiently explaining how we should hold a steering-wheel, and was being particularly well-wishing.

The road to the foster-home was passing through countryside. You could look out of the window, enthusiastically viewing herds of cows or old ladies with buckets drawing water from wells. I instantly perceived your tranquility and all the landscapes in your head arose in mine, too.

Our trip lasted for several hours. As we approached the foster home I became anxious and took you by the hand. Thoughts of our new dwelling frightened us, causing agitation because every time we knew for sure no one there would be glad to see us. Heavy rain with hail started and small pea-sized pieces of ice tapped on the windshield. Our lanky driver turned on screen-wipers. Soon a dim, lustrous light from the windows of an old, wooden hovel appeared ahead. As we approached, we saw a sleepy watchman who reluctantly looked out at the sight of our headlights. Without unnecessary questions he opened the gate, and we drove deep into an oak alley. In a minute, our voyage full of disturbing thoughts came to an end. We had arrived. The building of the foster home was exactly like I had imagined it: rather old, several storeys, white brick walls, grids on the ground-floor windows; and I also noticed several similar-looking buildings in the distance. The rain turned into a thin drizzle and the hail stopped. Our driver rummaged under a seat next to his, extracted an old, sloppy sheet and handed it to us.

"Well, perhaps you should cover yourself."

A middle-aged woman in a white robe with folds on her neck, a huge bust and sadness in her eyes came out of the building and, after a breezy conversation with the driver, asked for our papers, which he gave her.

"Follow me," she ordered in a monotonous, expressionless voice, glancing at our side without a shadow of curiosity. We flung a sheet on our shoulders, took our satchel and got out of the car.

"Well, bye, beast and beauty, have a good time," the lengthy fellow dropped as a good-bye to us, deftly jumped into the car and drove off with a sound of squeaking suspension. He must have been very anxious to see his Stakhanovite.

We slowly shuffled off through squelching slurry; our boots kept getting stuck. As we approached the building, in the windows I saw the faces of children who were attentively watching our every movement. The rain had almost stopped, but the dirty sheet was necessary for us to feel safe. It seemed to be capable of protecting us not only from bad weather but also from all kinds of trouble. Soon we stepped across the threshold and went up to the third floor. On our way we met two girls aged nearly fifteen; they looked at us with undisguised curiosity. One of them, a poor thing, was moving with evident difficulty, leaning her entire body on her friend's shoulder. For a moment I believed that we had come into a place where we were going to meet people similar in some way to ourselves and start a new, happy life. But... it lasted only a moment. Right ahead, a door with an inscription saying "Principal" told us where we were going. We timidly entered the room and saw a strikingly good-looking lady of about thirty-five sitting in state at a table. I have never seen such a beautiful woman before. I can still see her accurately picking sweets from a box with her graceful long fingers and, with her little finger sticking out, putting them into her mouth and sipping tea from her cup. She had a high forehead and huge blue eyes, bright, "shrilly", as if they were drawn in ink with a marker-pen. Her black hair coiled, set in a gorgeous, meticulous hairdo, her perfume smelled especially pleasant, but most amazing of all was exactly the same fold between her eyebrows as Lizzie had.

"Here are their documents from the boarding-school," a woman accompanying us reported, "a clinical record and a birth certificate."

The good-looking lady stared at us for some seconds in an accusatory and inquisitive fashion, flipping through our records at the same time, and then said:

"Well, well, Marfa Ilyinichna, what shall we do with them?"

Marfa shrugged her shoulders.

"Probably, treat and teach them, Inga Petrovna, just like everyone else."

"A zoo would be a better place for them, not this institution. That's where they could be of some use."

Her voice sounded quite icy, expressing disgust and hostility. Frowning, she ran her hand over her eyes several times as though getting used to the sight and finally added:

"What a repelling picture, indeed."

We felt very unwanted in her office, and Marfa also got confused and looked away.

"What garments am I supposed to give them? Ordinary clothes won't do. Shall I hire a special tailor for them? Does this marvel happen to have a name?"

All of a sudden you grew bolder and blurted out:

"Good afternoon, Inga Petrovna. My name is Hope, and she is Faith."

The principal gave us a sharp look that immediately accused us of all our past wrongdoings and of our future ones, too, including, first and foremost, the fact that we had had the audacity to be born, and chillily summarized:

"That's too long to keep in mind. You will be One, and you," she pointed at me, "you will be Two."

One, Two! Those were not even nicknames; those were just order-numbers or a count-off in military service. Somehow it reminded me of Lizzie once calling us Grace and Mystery. A lump came into my throat and I hardly restrained myself from bursting into tears there and then, right in the middle of her office.

"Well, all right, Marfa, take them to Pyotr Ilyich for initial examination, and then to the shower," the principal announced, "and after doing all that, get rid of this dirty rag they are covered with."

"Let's move out," Marfa ordered us with uncertainty.

Obviously, that Inga Petrovna didn't like us at all. I wished that nice lengthy fellow who had given us a lift was still with us. He had explained relativity with such vivid passion that now he would probably find the right words too. He might even start arguing with Inga Petrovna and convince her not to believe everything she saw and not to make hasty judgements on people she didn't know. But he was already far away, and we felt abandoned again.

Accompanied by Marfa Ilyinichna, we went down a long corridor, having no idea what was going to happen next, and our hearts bounced with uncertainty. Several times on our way we met boys and girls lingering between one room and the next without any point; some of them were completely grown-up. An absurd thought struck me: "What if gloomy Inga Petrovna and these kids in the corridor who seemed to imitate our awkward movements, as if on purpose, are just a dream?" But we were not sleeping. Many of the poor kids we met were diagnosed with terrible diseases like cerebral palsy. Some of them were getting about on crutches, others were carried in wheelchairs, but the majority were walking by themselves, dragging their disobedient feet. However, there were almost healthy children, too, who didn't have any noticeable disability and walked normally.

Pyotr Ilyich turned out to be a wrinkled, round-shouldered and very skinny old man. The dandruff on his shoulders resembled the traces of torn-off shoulder straps. Later we found out that he took part in the Great Patriotic War and was even given the Title of Hero. At the time of our arrival in the foster home, Pyotr Ilyich was over seventy years old but he didn't want to retire, claiming that his service to motherland was not over yet. He lived alone: his wife had died and his only daughter had moved to the capital city years ago.

Having shown a genuine interest in the surprising phenomenon before him, us, he walked three circles around us, crackling his knees, once clockwise and twice anticlockwise. He called us an "interesting case". And this was no fresh news – just words we had already heard before. Then he put us on weighing scales and cried out loud as if he was commanding a whole battalion advancing at the outset: "Oh my dear motherland! Together, you weigh exactly as much as my wife did; *a very interesting case, indeed*!" Saying this, he shook his head so energetically that his glasses slid down to the tip of his nose and the remains of his gray hair became shaggy and tumbled.

"Listen to my command!" he shouted again. "You will visit me once a week for control check-ups. Any questions?"

We nodded indecisively which meant yes and no at the same time. What if he was planning to dip us in cold water, or in boiling water which might be even worse? At the very thought of it I felt uneasy. I stared at the floor and blushed with anxiety.

"I understand that it will be no picnic for you here," said Pyotr Ilyich in a calmer voice. "Firstly, you are newbies, secondly, twins, and thirdly, conjoined — not merely something new but also something arrogant or mystical that strikes deep in the heart with irresistible force; it's likely to bother many people, but pluck up your spirits and you will be able to stand up for yourselves."

Suddenly something seemed to dawn on him and he started reminiscing, having nestled himself on the pressed-through chair.

"I have to tell you, things I've done in my past make me feel so ashamed and embarrassed, but there was one I am proud of. It happened not long after the war. I used to work in a hospital; that was lovely work for the benefit of our country. At that time our head physician died and a new one was put in charge. What a hang-by he was, not to say worse. He took all possible liberties: cracked dirty jokes, made passes at women who actually didn't mind at all. But when he started stretching his filthy paws to our kids, — just think about it: kids! — I couldn't stand it any longer. I got terribly mad and hit him in the belly, and then again and again until he began coiling on the floor like a grass snake. Oh, dear, it ended with real trouble. The Investigation Committee filed a case. I thought my life was over, but a wonderful thing happened. Was it somebody coming to my defense or was it a miracle? I can't say for sure, but I received good news: a higher authority was transferring me to this place. And here, life turned out to be not so bad. Things are tolerable, and, above all, I am needed and my work is of some use."

Pyotr Ilyich got so carried away with his story about the old days that he completely forgot we were still standing on the weighing scales; the sweet, forgetful, old man apparently did not know anything about the relativity of time or if he did, he had forgotten all about it.

Following his advice, I plucked up courage and opened my mouth to say something but he was ahead of me. "And now, girls, go straight to the showers. Double march!" he ordered and clapped his hands. Soon Marfa Ilyinichna, who was head of the women's department, came in and we went to the shower room.

Half an hour later we received two sets of identical clothes — our daily uniform. The trousers were too wide and were made of rough fabric; the top part represented two spacious gray shirts. Marfa helped us to get dressed without taking her eyes off the inscription in bold print behind our backs that was perceived to be offensive to the foster home management; then she handed us two pairs of boots, removed the obscenity from the wall, and gave a sigh of relief.

By the time we arrived in the dining room, it was already empty and all the children had gone back to their rooms long ago. For our supper we ate a plateful of potatoes with two scanty cutlets and two bowls of fish soup; although it contained no fish, we liked the soup the most. Meanwhile, Marfa was amiably chirping with the cook, an immense woman with square shoulders and wet half-circles of sweat on her robe under the armpits. She eventually noticed our empty plates and in an unexpectedly musical and tender voice addressed her rectangular companion with:

"Darling, bring them two teas."

Tea was made strong, brown, sour, unsugared. We noticed the dining room. It was impressive; it was as spacious as a genuine performance hall. And indeed, it became clear much later, sometimes nurses used it to dress up in fancy gowns and high-heel shoes. They even organized real dance evenings on the premises, in order to chase away boredom.

Right after we had finished our tea, Marfa literally pushed us into a large, white room and closed the door tight. Fully grown-up girls were sitting or reclining on beds, and several guys were sitting at the table. Everybody was gazing at us without a word. It always happens that way: first, people examine us closely, then usually reflect upon something for a very long while. At last, one of the girls got up and, loudly shuffling her feet, walked right up to us. She was seemingly seventeen, red-haired, freckled, with a fleshy nose and small, deep-set eyes; clumping on the floor, she dragged her left foot.

"What a hoot! I can't take my eyes off them. They look like a real, two-headed, little dragon," she burst out laughing, and circled us quickly. I guess it was a sort of acquaintance-ritual at the place. "Totally crippled. How could they possibly have been born?"

"You'd better ask them," one of the guys grinned through his teeth. "Although it's clear how."

"But how can they even live looking like this?" she muttered.

"Watch it at the back or at the front, it's still the same," the other guy recited. "Two heads, four arms, four legs and one ass."

"You are a real poet," the red-haired girl exclaimed. "So, what nickname did the principal grant you?" she addressed us again. "Y-shaped? Brigade?"

"My name is Faith," I said, "and this is Hope".

"Keep that for inscribing in your copybooks. Everybody here has a name that Inga Petrovna, or Adolf's Daughter, or Adoter, for short, as we call her, *deems proper*. Just beware not to blurt out what we call her in her presence. Clear? So what are your *new* names?"

31

My tongue didn't move and seemed to stick to the top of my palate. But you spat out:

"One-Two."

For several seconds everybody pondered, then everyone fell about, laughing.

"Well, Adoter has played quite a trick," choking with laughter, one of girls squeezed out through tears.

"Come on, quit cackling," we heard from the right corner. "We are all flawed here. At least they can walk, so we will have someone to empty bedpans."

"Shut up, stupid, and keep your advice to yourself or for your boyfriend when you're in bed with him," the red-haired one responded. "And we kept wondering why they prepared just one bed for two of them. And here they are! Everybody calls me Sprinter, because I'm the fastest of all walking CCP's[6] but, according to my passport, I am Olga Petrovna. The adviser from the corner is called Godly Girl and outside this place her name's Marinka. Later, you will get acquainted with the others. So, why are you standing and staring? Take a seat over there." And she pointed to a chair near the door.

We were tired so we went to the chair and sat down. A flimsy chair fractured cracking, and we crashed down on to the floor, falling on our backs. Frantic laughter ran through the room. I felt the full depth of our disgrace. I wanted to hide in the corner and wrap myself in an old sheet. We resembled a messy knot of arms and legs on that cold floor, and the whole scene was oppressive.

However, this humiliation only made you feel more and more indignant. Helping me up and rubbing your own injured parts, you maliciously squawked aloud through clenched teeth:

---

6   Slang - children suffering from cerebral palsy.

"Are you happy now? And when did you last look at yourselves in a mirror?"

Your words had an immediate effect. The laughter stopped. One of the guys even rose from the table and removed the broken chair.

Godly Girl stood up for us again:

"Why did you get them on the bottom? Can't you see they are totally miserable? If you cripple them by accident, more than they're already crippled, you'll pay for it."

"All right," muttered Sprinter in a conciliatory way, "the guys are simply fooling around; the chair *incidentally* happened to be broken. Here is your bed, the empty one next to Half-Jane's; it will definitely bear your weight." And she pointed with her finger at a newly made bed near the wall opposite the window. Later we knew that our neighbor Half-Jane — that skinny creature with pale, yellowish skin and thin, greasy hair — was completely paralysed from the waist down.

"Please don't blame it all on us," one of the guys, the "poet" with a wooden artificial leg, responded. "Who could imagine that they are stuck together? Go figure it out with them hiding under that sheet. Will you have some vodka?"

We cautiously reached our bed, stepping indecisively as if on thin ice. I was staggering rather than walking, holding my hurt side. Guys poured a muddy liquid from a bottle into a glass and handed it to us. You sipped a half glass at one dash, shrank, then moved your shoulders and bit the slice of bread they generously handed over to you; I mistrustfully drank up the remains. We got tipsy at once, lay down and covered ourselves with a blanket, not having the slightest wish to talk.

Over time it became clear that booze-ups were arranged quite often. Everybody was drinking and practically forcing one another to drink. At times it is so enjoyable to mire your neighbor with the same filth you have been stuck in for so long! They hid bottles under their pillows or in boots and sometimes piled them up behind a locker. At night all the bottles were collected, brought to the kitchen and carefully camouflaged under potato peel. There were many ways to disguise the drinking, but the kitchen was the most popular option.

"Bad luck for you; this is not just a lousy foster-home; it's the worst I've ever lived in. Everyone here is a poor cripple with a scary diagnosis," stated one of the guys, a sturdy fellow nicknamed Seamstress, with a long, ugly, sewn-up scar under his right eye. I couldn't get rid of one thought which occupied my mind even under the influence: what piggish nicknames everybody had in that place. They put more dishonor on to the already burdened than on to anyone else. Good-looking but furious principal, stupid caregivers, repulsive chow — all we are given and all we have. I must say that the teachers are quite OK, but they don't give a damn about anything. They come, chatter their lessons and buzz off. It is not so bad in our building, almost everybody can walk, but the neighboring building is a total nightmare; there the bed-ridden fellows lie; the stench of death is there."

"And God be with them," Godly Girl put in a word.

"But it doesn't mean that people began to talk more," Sprinter interrupted her public confession and asked us: "Have you got parents or are you from a children's home?"

"Have got parents," I answered through a drunken haze.

"So why did they put you in here?"

"Whoever would want to have them by their side?" the poet grinned.

"So, you're from a children's home," Sprinter cheered up, solving the puzzle and then tried to create the suitable scenario for herself. "The right girls in the right place. Seamstress, pour another round."

It sometimes feels like you and I are at the movie theater, sitting next to each other and watching the same movie. People say something, argue incessantly, even fight, but it is all somewhere else, somewhere far away, on the other side of the screen, and we are just passive onlookers unable to affect the course of events.

At ten we heard a loud announcement – bedtime, and the lights in the rooms were turned off. The boys unwillingly got up, promptly said goodnight and left the room, taking the remains of the alcohol with them.

I cried the entire first night, stuffing a corner of the pillow into my mouth so that nobody could hear me. I was miserable, to say the least. That was the day I really felt like a *creep* for the first time.

"It is not worth worrying about something you can't change," you said after I had calmed down. "Even the worst things go away sooner or later."

I recalled your advice whenever I felt down and began to believe that one day our suffering would come to an end.

Injustice as
a Standard of Living

The reveille announcement was accompanied by the same lively buzzer as bedtime. A sharp arrow of the round clock hit seven. Someone from personnel turned on the radio. The vigorous voice of an announcer confirmed the precise time and started speaking cheerfully, awakening our vast country, and meanwhile emphasizing how many happy moments there had been in the past and how many there still were ahead of us. Then he reluctantly finished broadcasting and gave way to a program of morning exercises. I felt ashamed, awkward, offended because I suddenly realized that waking up at eight in the boarding school, we were left behind by the whole country. While I was reflecting on this, nurses pushed a wheelchair to the neighboring bed where Half-Jane was lying. She humbly smiled at them and drove away as if in time with the music. Meanwhile, Marfa Ilyinichna flitted into the room and squalled noisily but with a bit of insecurity:

"All rise! To the bathroom, hurry up, then morning-exercises. And don't make me say it twice!"

Because I was only half awake, we clumsily dragged ourselves to the washbasins where in no time at all we had been turned into an object for everyone's curiosity. Well, indeed we are champions at that.

"Oh, my sin, I thought that you were a delusion yesterday," Godly Girl's flat face with its snub nose and hollow cheeks shined in a smile. "Got any tooth powder?"

"Yes," we nodded and shared the powder with her.

"I hate mornings! These habitual, standard, useless exercises Nag forces us to do," she said through the bubbling tooth powder in her mouth. "And the procedures... anyway, God be with them, we cannot avoid them since they are compulsory."

"I hate the procedures, too. Why the devil do they have these procedures if they are of no damn use?" the second neighbor said, meanwhile popping pimples on her face with trembling hands. "I was born crooked and I am gonna die that way. Why are they giving me these damn shots and making me undergo these sessions like a convict sentenced to hard labor? God Damn it!"

"Stop saying "damn it." Godly Girl uttered, spitting out tooth powder into the shabby sink. Further conversation made no sense, and everyone went about his or her own business.

The most trivial visit to the lavatory turned into an unbearable torture; it was unreal to get used to the stench eating into our nostrils like ammonia spirit. Since we were given the status of "newcomers", we were the last in the line, and for nearly a quarter of an hour were inhaling the aromas of earlier excrement. Of course, as a result, we were late for the morning exercises. At first we cautiously covered several flights of stairs, and then trudged through the long corridor like a mad turtle – two mad turtles – in an effort to join the rest as soon as possible. Approaching the gym, we heard incessant whistling sounds – furious, commanding, hysterical – constantly interrupted by sharp bawls of Nag's voice.

"Here, listen to my command. Start marching in line. Move it, move it, loonies! Keep the distance. No leaning on each other, no flocking, lengthen your stride. Hey, I said, lengthen your stride, whimpers! Stand still... One... Two! Hands up, breathe in, hands down, breathe out. Breathe! Breathe with your chest. Your chest, slackers! And now let's proceed to squats. And down, and up, and down, and up. Come on, get down, quick! I said get down, not bend."

A strange atmosphere reigned in the gym. An ordinary, average-looking woman sat solemnly on a high chair in the center of the premise. She had a magic whistle hanging on her neck that seemed to live a life of its own. A bunch of kids gathered around her. Among them we saw our drinking companions from yesterday now turned into obedient puppets by the worn-out whistle. Some of them did exercises rather easily: some guys sluggishly bent their bodies, trying to squat, others inclined their heads intensely and awkwardly bent their knees, but the majority made movements I won't even begin to describe. It resembled hysterics rather than morning exercises: children squirmed, coiled, kinked and jittered as if they were mocking each other in a grotesque play. The sight could really get on your nerves. Those exercises introduced us to the entire range of musculoskeletal disorders.

"Double march! Go, go!" Nag and her whistle ordered. "Step forward, don't hobble. I wish you were out of my sight, Quasimodos."

She could have been the perfect radio announcer. I thought she could have woken the dead. Finally, Agafia Petrovna (that was this lovely woman's name) noticed us.

"Are you waiting for a special invitation?"

She didn't even turn an eyelash when she saw us; she was so deeply involved in the exercises.

"Fall in, quickly! I'm counting up to two: One... Two."

Girls from our room laughed in unison. Without further delay, we joined the rank and file.

"Quicken your pace. Hurry up, move it!" she encouraged the trainees with a fighting spirit until her sight fell on one poor guy: "Hey, you, cack-handed skinny-minnie, why are you poking your claws in everybody's snout? Hey, I'm talking to you. Be sure, I'm gonna remember your ugly face and teach you a lesson. Ok, turn around and march in the opposite direction. Quicker, raise your knees and no shirking, badger-legged, I said, no simulating. Stand still. One…Two!" What a brisk lady, real sportswoman and member of the 'Komsomol'7.

I felt with my entire body how diligently you were trying to do all the exercises and repeated after you, sincerely regretting the ten minutes we had lost because of our lateness. Training-time passed quickly. We soon found ourselves in the breakfast room.

As usual, we occupied two chairs. They served us oatmeal with butter and tea. Everybody seemed to have gotten accustomed to our appearance; only Sprinter glanced at our side inquisitively from time to time because when we were sitting at the table we looked like two normal people of independent status.

Leaving the dining room, we ran into Marfa Ilyinichna at the door.

"Pyotr Ilyich concludes that you don't have any serious diseases. He only prescribed you electrophoresis and physical activity."

Without answering we went to the physiotherapy room. Fortunately, the procedure was absolutely painless. In the treatment room we saw a pretty, young nurse. She had probably

---

7   Young Communist League.

been notified of our visit in advance because she behaved dispassionately and didn't even look at us. She subtly waved her hand, pointing to the couch. Then, still silently, she approached the couch, turned on a massive device standing nearby and attached some stickers with wires to our bodies. However, she did speak two phrases:

"There are always such unfortunate kids in the population. I feel so sorry for them."

Then she sighed impassively and went to another part of the room.

Physical education class was held in the same gym, by the same Agafia Petrovna Nag; it turned out to be her real last name. All the CCP's hated her and from time to time made secret raids attempting to steal or damage her magic whistle, but all in vain – an old and fairly chipped whistle, apparently, had grown into her body, her life and her soul. To cut a long story short, all the kids were bending, running, squatting for forty-five minutes, having a pretty hard time. I couldn't keep pace with you, missed the pace, my body ached and disobeyed me, but I don't regret the time we spent performing Nag's exercises. They helped us in the long run.

After that, we had to go to school located in a nearby building where our academic knowledge was tested.

"No cheating," the Russian language and literature teacher repeated several times during the dictation, "and no disturbing your neighbor with your elbows."

Should I mention how difficult it is for us to find a convenient position at a school desk in order not to "disturb the neighbor with our elbows"? I was ready to hear, "No cheating off your *neighbor*, or I'll seat you at separate desks," but the teacher of Russian language and literature had compassion for us. After all, she was a humanities-minded person.

Weird things continued to happen in that maths class. The teacher who was walking on tiptoes turned severely pale when we moved towards him, and stretched his hand forward, as if he was trying to push us aside; meanwhile, he took off and put on his glasses automatically with the other hand. We were solving one mathematical problem together and writing the solution on the blackboard while he nodded, "Right, right, sure. No doubt," nervously wiping his forehead with a handkerchief and coughing slightly.

A history class was cancelled because the teacher got sick.

When Adoter was shown the results of our tests, she laughed long and loud. It appeared that you were supposed to stay in the seventh grade for a second time while I had made it to the eighth. On a special form she set forth her order, according to which both of us were to stay in the seventh grade. After that we went to lunch with a light heart. We had a green borsch for the first course, mashed potatoes with peas for the second course, and seniors' protest for the dessert. Some of them tapped their spoons on the table, others trampled their feet, and everybody refused to eat.

"Why is everyone refusing food?" I inquired.

"Adoter prohibited smoking in the rooms. The kids are furious about it," Godly Girl explained. "This is how they express their disagreement."

"She deprives us of something she hasn't got the slightest idea about," Sprinter said, loudly. "You can't survive here without smokes. On to the barricades! You're gonna be a tank," she encouraged us and started cackling loudly. People are strange and incomprehensible. Once they are forbidden from doing something, they revolt, growing loud and unrestricted in their hate. That's why even non-smoking kids participated in the dining-room strike.

We went back to our room and sat on our bed. We had a lot of work to do to reshape two pairs of trousers, shirts and pyjamas, for which they gave us some thread and needles along with the clothes. On the near bed, Half-Jane was sitting, reading a book, a silly, timid smile on her face, flat like a palm. Thoughts of books were constantly coming into our heads.

"Excuse me, is there a library here?" I wondered naively, forgetting about fixing the clothes.

"Downstairs, on the first floor. But it is an extremely boring place where you can get nothing but Soviet propaganda and all kinds of nonsense about the school reading program."

Meanwhile, Sprinter headily tottered into the room. She was still outraged.

"How dare that bitch forbid us anything that is *natural*? So, what next? No eating, no sleeping, no having kids?"

By the way, Adoter had no children and, apparently, not knowing what else to do, she devoted all her spare time to our foster home.

"I hate that damned wretch," Sprinter couldn't calm down, "especially when you go into her office and there she sits and chews her sweets calmly, not even swallowing them, and then spits out the sweet mush into the trash bin. Have you seen that yet?"

We nodded.

"She guzzles them in our presence *on purpose* because she wants us to drool over them. Her husband gets her those imported sweets through his connections; he's some sort of a big gun. He's got a private car and a country house and all that crap. Anyway, you will sneak into her office and take one sweet from the box. I have decided!"

"What for?"

"To restore justice. This will be your chance to help me, after which you will join our gang. Cripples like you could be of use. Now, got it, One-Two? I will teach you how to pull the deal."

"We have never stolen anything before," I tried to protest. "And if you know how to do it, why don't you do it yourself?"

"That's it," said red-haired Sprinter getting enraged. "I've eaten too much shit here already for some four-legged sheep to tell me what to do."

"Leave them alone," Half-Jane cut in sadly.

"And who on earth is asking you for an opinion, you limbless dumb?" Sprinter cut her short and addressed us again. "Half-Jane is so stupid she doesn't even get how ugly you are and what you're going to go through because of it. But I *know* and I wanna take care of you. You help me and I'm gonna help you; I will take you under my wing; it's all fair. Consider it a test."

"How do we do it?" you showed an interest.

"Every evening after work Adoter leaves her office keys with the concierge, a half-deaf old woman of about eighty. You just appear before her the way you are, and the old hag's going to freak out till she's blue in the face. Or maybe she'll peg out for real, that'll be fun!" Sprinter paused for a moment to check the impression her words were making, but for some reason there was no reaction. "Kidding. She's gonna survive, that scumbag," she flung out almost disappointedly. "She's too tough to die. Well, you should do your best to distract the creaker; meanwhile, Snot will snitch the keys."

And she waved her hand towards the window near which the youngest dweller of the room was husking sunflower seeds. I would guess her age to be eleven; there was nothing remarkable about her appearance except her scrawny figure.

"We will do the trick in the evening, and now, get lost."

She spoke of our "ugliness" as though it was a normal, everyday occurrence, without any restriction on her choice of words. I felt bitterly hurt deep in my soul (yet again) and was prepared to turn down her request, but you took my hand and squeezed it firmly. Then I understood: you wanted us to steal a sweet from the box; and I didn't have the nerve to object. We always humble ourselves before bastards and it has become a habit. So, after rummaging in a built-in cabinet, Sprinter took out a small cardboard-box, called up Snot and Ragbag – a hefty girl with a pink face and huge arms – and the three of them left the room.

"You don't have any chance to beat Sprinter because half the girls will join up with her," Half-Jane shared her thoughts in a low voice. "Making friends with her is impossible too and, to be honest, pointless."

"Where have they gone?" I asked her.

"They're going to pour glue into buckets."

"What's that for?"

"It's their revenge for the downtrodden honor; so sensitive have they become," Half-Jane continued willingly. "An incident happened last week: cleaners brought their children to work with them so that the young brats could help them to wash the walls, and one of our guys caught their attention. They surrounded him in a semicircle and began mocking or, to be precise, gloating over the fact that they were born healthy and he was a cripple."

She sniffed in contempt, moved her shoulders and proceeded with her reading.

"I think they didn't care that he was a cripple," I said. "They just grabbed the chance to bully someone."

"Well, very naturally, children are always careless," Half-Jane remarked sarcastically. "They just treat everyone like pee, especially cripples."

People have no limits either in love or in hatred. But is it their fault? They despise us because they are afraid, for we remind them that getting crippled or sick might happen to anyone; or, perhaps, the true reason for their hatred lies much deeper inside, stemming from a hidden ugliness in their souls?

We got to our first class early. The number of school-desks in that huge classroom nearly tripled the number of students. At three o'clock sharp, a history teacher appeared who was said to be sick, but she didn't look sick at all. She wrote today's date, month and year in the top, right-hand corner of the blackboard, after which she dispassionately sat at her desk and started shouting out our last names to check attendance. After the check-up she seemed to calm down, glanced at us and asked icily:

"Does anyone notice what's wrong?"

A deathly silence in the class. I thought she might be talking about us, meaning that *we* were something *wrong*, and in my mind I prepared to put up with further mockery. Meanwhile, the history teacher became extremely upset and finally declared:

"Today is the twelfth of September, and what date is on the blackboard?"

"The fourteenth of December," reasoned Godly Girl.

"Then would you be so kind as to rise and write the date correctly?"

Godly Girl got up and, hobbling guiltily, dragged herself to correct the "mistake". It was the first time we were in such a situation. For forty-five long minutes I was tormented by the question: If the first lesson begins with an intentional mistake, then how can we possibly believe anything we study in that history class?

During recreation between Russian language and mathematics classes, some bullyboy who looked like an overgrown child tripped us. I badly bruised my knee and we limped for the rest of the day, leaning to my side clumsily.

"Hope, I wonder if they understand that we obviously feel exactly the way they feel when healthy children make fun of them?"

"They don't, Faith," you answered. "In their eyes, we are not poor cripples deserving compassion, but just a two-headed freak they hate and fear."

You have always seen people in their true colors, without any illusions, not hoping for anything. As for me, I still can't manage to understand why even such a ridiculous animal as an ant-eater or a desman can get people's sympathy and affection, *but not us*? Perhaps they just haven't got used to us yet?

I often wondered what it would be like – having your own body, going where you wanted, doing what you liked doing. How does it feel not being the hostage of somebody else, even if it is your closest and dearest relative? It was determined by nature that you make the first choice in all our decisions. Our minute difference in height sorted things out: intuitively I have always had to adjust to you and your desires. During our free time when we were supposed to go for a walk or play games, we had to decide where to go and what to do. When one of us was in a bad mood, felt drowsy or needed to weep, both of us were confined to bed. In the boarding school we were physically inactive and quite seldom able to socialize with our peers; here, our life was supposed to be pretty much the same. But when we started talking about the library, both of us got really excited. Our excitement and curiosity made us think it was the place where we might find answers to all our questions. What if someone had already faced a problem similar to ours and had already written a book about it? What if there was actually a *great variety* of people just like us scattered around the world and incapable of meeting each other and uniting? The library acquired a special significance for us, and without further ado we were off to it. We searched for relevant information for several hours, but, unfortunately, our search proved fruitless; however, we found a vast abundance of other interesting books. Is it worth mentioning how dramatically Half-Jane was mistaken? The library represented the true adornment of the foster-home. But most of all, I remembered the librarian, a slovenly-looking woman nearing forty with intense streaks of gray in her hair and a sharply pointed, long nose. I had no doubts at all that the foster kids would nickname her Pinocchia if they happened to visit the library just once in their lives.

She always recommended books by truly good and genuine writers, and poets.

"One guy happened to come here quite often previously; he was very fond of reading. So, he marked the places that he liked the most in books. It was about ten years ago, at the commencement of my work here. I was inexperienced and didn't forbid him to scratch books with his nail, thinking: "All right, that's no big deal, no one comes here". Poor guy was feeling much worse than you: he couldn't move, was shaking all over as if he was feverish, and his speech was inarticulate."

"And where is he now?" we exclaimed in the same breath.

"He was transferred to a nursing home, where he soon passed away asleep at the age of nineteen as was discovered later. It may sound strange, but he had a good death," she remarked thoughtfully. "Well, all right, enjoy your reading, but don't damage anything."

A good death at the age of nineteen, it sounds terrible! But perhaps, at some point in time, those who are living *without a body* want nothing more. And the more surprising it was to see his marks, those dead traces stretching throughout the library books like a web; and sometimes in the margin we found his illegible scribble – thoughtful judgments that survived their author? He used to read a lot, reflect on things, had a desire to live though he realized there was not much time left to him. At times I imagined him sitting at the nearest desk, concentrating, flipping the pages and, after finishing the book, joyfully dancing on the desk with his fingers – *fingers only.*

We wanted to stay in the library as long as possible, but closing time came, so we said goodbye to the librarian and left for supper.

Everybody was eating with evident pleasure, including the instigators of the lunchtime strike, and we gladly joined them. In the dining room Sprinter stayed clear of us and didn't even look our way, but once we returned to the room, she immediately interfered in our life. She called us over with a rude gesture; Snot was fidgeting in the corner, on her bed.

"Adoter made tracks long ago; the oldster woman is idling around at the reception desk. Payback time has come. And don't even try to hide under that sheet so that the devil only can sort out what you really are!"

After saying "devil", she aggressively looked askew at Godly Girl sitting nearby. The latter did not react in her usual way, and Sprinter continued:

"So listen. You should approach the cubbyhole where the concierge keeps her keys trying to stay unnoticed, and then ask suddenly but quite casually, "Where's the library?" If she doesn't pop off the hooks that very moment, she will move her ass out into the corridor to show you the way."

"But the library is already closed," I uttered indistinctly.

"Doesn't matter, the old hag is feeble-minded and sluggish. As soon as she leaves her desk, Snot will pull the keys and pass them to you, and you'll move fast and open the office. And take your sister with you, just in case."

My soul was burning with disagreement, but despite that, we nodded one after the other and were off to commit the deed. Everything went just as Sprinter had planned and even better. When the concierge saw us, she screamed and, blinking convulsively, came close to us.

"Who are you, and who do you think you are?" she gabled with a glimpse of curiosity on her sorrowful, aged face.

"Where is the library? We were told to return a book," you rapped out, while I was anxiously imagining our "brilliant" plan falling to pieces like a sandcastle. But the concierge, to my astonishment, kindly accompanied us to the library doors, even though it was a quarter to ten in the evening! Now we were ready to perform the most impudent and senseless deed of our life – to steal a sweet from a box of chocolates. I didn't believe that it was happening for real until I saw a familiar inscription "Principal" before my eyes, and the only key from the office was already in my hand.

For a while that hand, my hand, hesitated near the keyhole.

"Why have you stopped?" you began to worry. "Time's passing. What if somebody walks along the corridor right now and catches us in the act?"

"This is stealing".

"It's just a sweet".

"A stolen sweet, and now you and I are thieves."

"On the other hand, we will have a *family* and all the bullies will finally back off. Or maybe you like being abused?"

"Of course I don't, but..."

"Then let's do it for our own sake," you hurried to encourage me.

We turned the key in the lock and entered in confusion, closing the door behind us. It was very dark in the office and we had to make our way by touch until our eyes got used to the dark. The box of chocolates, lonely lying on the table, seemed gray and unnatural. I opened a paper cover and took a sweet at random. At any other time, I would have given a lot just to taste it, but at that moment... standing one step away from the so much desired sweets, I hated them. I was already closing the box when you threw your wide-spread hand forward and seized another sweet.

"Let's take two. An extra one in case we can't keep ourselves from tasting the first one."

The lights in the corridor were off, but our eyes had already got used to the dark; anyway, we held on to the wall in order not to stumble. Soon we would reach the staircase leading down to the second floor, and we would be done...

All of a sudden we heard a groan coming from the women's bathroom, intermittently tailing off and then repeating itself. I was curious and worried: somebody *obviously* needed help. You pulled the handle. The door creaked open, giving in, rubbing the floor. There was a bedpan put behind the door from the inside, and I tumbled over it when I walked in. The door accidentally opened wide, and a bright, dazzling light rushed out into the corridor. I closed my eyes tight for a second or two but before doing so I had already noticed what was happening. A huge guy with his trousers down was standing with his back to us, pressing his whole body towards the nurse who had done the electrophoresis-procedure for us in the morning; she was groaning in his arms. I recognized him at once: crooked legs, ears with no lobes – actually, he had lobes but they merged into his cheekbones by a weird freak of nature – and a wrinkled, baby-like nape. It was Wash'em Clean, that guy from the tenth grade who had tripped us up during the break .

"You da-damned ba-ba-stards, now I'm really gonna k-k-crack your heads op-pen," he mumbled, turning back his head and thrusting his left shoulder forward, while picking up his pants with short, muscled arms.

We instantly closed the door and started instinctively stepping backwards until we bumped up against a wall. Fear was dimming our thoughts, taking them off what we had just seen. We cut through the staircase and the corridor in one dash – that was as good as impossible in our case – and literally flew head over heels into our room. After getting our breath back and recovering from what we had just seen, we tiptoed up to Sprinter's bed, trying not to wake anybody.

"Did everything go well?" she hissed at us to be quiet, which was quite unnecessary.

I rummaged in my pocket and handed a sweet over to her without a word. She took it with apparent indifference, throwing it negligently to one side:

"And you didn't lose the keys, did you?"

I must admit, I got frightened. Well, it was more abashment than fear; I merely felt awkward and annoyed. My mind swarmed with absurd thoughts: "Did I take the keys? Did I close the office door?" We started digging in our pockets convulsively, but instead of the keys you took out the second sweet by mistake.

"You're such bitches!" Sprinter nearly choked with indignation. "You totally screwed up. I asked for one, One-Two. Two is too obvious."

"We did it by mistake; each of us took one," you said without blinking. "It was dark and we couldn't see."

"We wanted to taste one, too," I tried to excuse us, "but later, not in the principal's office."

Our strikingly dissimilar behavior seemed to confound Sprinter. She probably thought we *always did and said the same thing*. She couldn't get her mind round our dissimilar versions.

Staring at us, she seemed to be chewing on silence. Her lips were moving but no words were coming out. Then suddenly,

"I see, you decided to act out of sync. Are you conjoined for real or just faking it for everyone's displeasure?"

Instead of answering, I handed her the key which was in my pocket.

"All right, get off to sleep. Snot, come here."

We wearily made our way to bed. Half-Jane was not asleep; leaning on a pillow, she was watching the scene without any evident interest.

"You're swift. Anyway, it's not surprising, since you've got four legs; I wish you could give me one at least. What's the use of all four?" and a meek smile flitted across her face. "How did everything go?"

Whispering and interrupting each other, we told her everything, not omitting the strange incident or scene in the bathroom.

"Gee, you're totally naive; you don't know anything at all about lovemaking, do you?"

We exchanged glances, thoughtful.

"Of course we do." You sounded offended.

Yes, we were aware of what happens between girls and boys when they're crazy about each other. Some of them talked about their escapades for hours. But listening to stories and seeing things with your own eyes are quite different. The only thing I felt at that moment was an overwhelming, all-encompassing disgust.

"But why do two people in love do that if it hurts?"

"You're so dumb, One-Two! Were you born in a cave or what?" Catching her breath after the first bout of laughter, Half-Jane asked, "Who told you tales that it hurts? Well, maybe it is not a big pleasure either, but it's so beautiful," she added doubtfully.

"Have you tried it yourself or do you know everything from hearsay?" you wondered.

Not even deigning to answer but only humming her contempt, Half-Jane hid her head under the blanket and started snoring loudly. Soon you fell asleep, too, but I lay awake for a long time thinking about what I had seen. After all, if people do it, it must be good for them.

The next morning turned out to be an identical copy of the one before and all the subsequent mornings we had to spend in the foster home. As always, we stood in a line for the lavatory, though now we were not the last to go in. We brushed our teeth, had breakfast, did morning exercises. In short, we got into an endless loop and there was seemingly no way out of it.

At the beginning of morning exercises, Adoter entered the gym accompanied by Marfa Ilyinichna and the old concierge. A silence fell, being occasionally interrupted by irregular breathing from an exhausted "athlete".

"Last night an incident occurred within our walls," Adoter started. "Somebody stole the keys at the reception desk, broke into my office and rummaged through my personal belongings. And I have grounds to believe that it was one of you. Whoever did it, he or she will be punished."

"Holy crap, Adoter must have counted all her sweets," Snot standing next to us whispered. Some of the kids gave a silent whistle.

"I already have an idea who it was," the principal continued. "I suggest the culprit confesses voluntarily; in that case, the punishment will be less severe."

She spoke calmly, but her eyes flared with rage, looking even more beautiful than usual. For several moments we were captivated by this look, wondering how a perfectly evil spirit and beauty can combine in one person, each harmoniously supplementing the other.

Nobody made a move, and I couldn't get rid of the thought that she was looking at us.

"Well, if nobody is going to admit his guilt, I will have to look through your personal belongings, and believe me, the one who committed this crime is going to regret it very much. And now carry on with your morning exercises, quickly."

My teeth chattered with fear, though I knew she couldn't find any evidence. Sprinter stealthily approached us from behind and muttered:

"If you point at me, I will let you rot!" I wanted to run away and hide, but you wouldn't move. The physical education class continued.

When Adoter and Marfa Ilyinichna came into our room, all the girls were standing near their beds. The head of the department methodically turned out the contents of our bedside tables, and the principal scanned them with her X-ray-like eyes. After a fruitless search they called a caregiver and started moving beds away from the walls. While Adoter rummaged underneath searching for a sweet wrapper, Marfa stood looking around, fidgeting with her foot.

"Well, here is the guilty one!" joyfully exclaimed Adoter. She picked up a wrapper lying under Sprinter's bed with her two long nails which resembled a pair of tweezers.

"We have to do something," I whispered to you and blurted out aloud at once: "She's not guilty. I did it."

"You did? Then why is this here?" And the principal pointed at the crumpled sweet-wrapper.

"I dumped it there."

Trying to suppress my fear, I hastily rapped out my confession as if declaiming a poem by heart.

"I stole the key, burgled the office, took several sweets out of the box, ate them, and then returned the key to the reception desk. I didn't take anything else, and there was nobody there except me. My sister is not guilty!" That was an absurd admission in our case.

Adoter listened coldly and gloomily and obviously did not believe a single word, but she could do nothing. She knew that the concierge had seen only the two of us, and the story about the sweets was irritating her more and more.

"You are going to have a very hard time in our friendly collective," she said, frowning, "both of you."

Pausing for a moment, she gave us time to prepare for what she was about to say. Then, as if being afraid that she would not be heard, she declared loudly:

"The guilty ones will receive their punishment, that is, ten days in the isolation cell, with attendance of all necessary studies."

"What kind of punishment is that if we have to go to classes?" I thought in the back of my mind.

As strange as it may seem, teenagers tried not to lag behind the school curriculum. Satisfactory marks helped us to enroll at technical school and even university, avoiding nursing homes or nut hospitals[8]. However, this only applied to walking kids; bed-ridden patients were penalized from the word "go".

We left the room in silence, without any thoughts. The sentence had been given and arguing made no sense at all. However, I did not feel guilty, maybe because I had made a confession and re-established my own sense of justice. Only one thing was confusing me. In order to find a family in a place where nobody cares about you, you are supposed to commit

---

8   Slang - mental hospital.

a crime first, and then voluntarily endure punishment. First, you cave in striving for a better destiny, and then you have to give up your life. And what do you receive in return? A clear conscience? But isn't your conscience clearer *without committing a misdemeanor*?

"Hurry up," the principal ordered. "You must move more quickly than the others. After all, you have four legs, not just two. And all four of them are healthy."

Why does everybody care so much about our four legs? Is it envy or what?

And what is there to say about Marfa Ilyinichna, the head of the women's department? That woman, chary of words and emotions, only seemed to exist to provide everybody with a *perfect* example of resigned, meek submission to every whim of her chief; she only sighed when she had to call us by our names. Faceless and gray, not even given a nickname, she walked slowly, shrinking her head into her shoulders as if ashamed of the awkward scenes she took part in. I expected her to say at least a couple of words of support and understanding but she continued to maintain a deadly silence in the corridor, on the staircase and outside. Only at the door of the low, wooden accessory-building, looking like a hen-house, did she force herself to say a trivial "Come in", addressing either us or Adoter.

We entered a small room, which turned out to be dark and damp inside. A light was switched on. The first thing to strike the eye was a dirty floor and shabby walls. Marfa stood at the door for a while and then indecisively nodded to a small bed, saying, "Have a rest," and slowly walked out.

"Have a rest." Very funny!

Adoter didn't even budge.

Left alone, we sat in silence for a long time, each of us absorbed in her own thoughts.

"Don't be upset," you said at last, trying to encourage me. "Some time all of this will come to an end."

"I hope so," I said.

Suddenly, an incredible thought came into my mind.

"Hope," I started, "what if initially they had named you Faith and me Hope, but afterwards they forgot which of us was which and swapped our names around by mistake? You always believe that everything is going to be all right, and your faith helps me."

"And you hope that it will be that way. We have this close bond between us." After thinking a while, you added, "All people need hope; no one can live without it; and our hope is way stronger when it is warmed up by faith. So it isn't really important who is Faith and who is Hope; the main thing is that *we are connected together*."

And we hugged each other, sitting on our bed in our "corrective apartment".

Every day "benevolent" Marfa came to bring us to classes, seated us at a distant desk, and after the classes escorted us back to the isolation cell and locked the door behind us. Our food was delivered directly "to our bed". Time hung intolerably heavy, like the day we'd stood on the weighing scales in Pyotr Ilyich's office, but after ten days we didn't want to leave. We seemed to have grown deeply attached to our musty, rag-filled room.

Kittens in a Bag

When we returned to our usual room, nobody said a word about what had happened. Everyone forgot quite successfully how we had stolen sweets and then had taken all the blame for the sake of Sprinter. Of course, we didn't gain the family we had been promised. I expected them to say at least a couple of words of thanks, but there weren't any. Since that day we have never set eyes on the nurse who did electrophoresis; rumor has it that she got a job elsewhere. Our life turned into one long, meaningless day, and every following year was no different from the previous one. But nevertheless there were some changes that seemed unnoticeable: the meals were getting worse and worse and the CCP's more and more rackety and mean. They boozed up with the personnel without scruple, arranged frequent drinking parties at night in the gym, and blatantly skipped classes, not forgetting to mock us in their spare time. We spent most of our time in the library, hiding from our so-called family. Nobody ever peeped into the reading room, and we could sit there quietly for hours reading books or flipping through pages, sometimes for no reason at all. Soon you began smoking, and I, previously having been categorically opposed to this addiction, followed your lead after six months. We obtained cigarettes by washing others' clothes with our four hands.

Literally, from the very first day in the foster home, we had got the message: the more miserable a victim was, the more ruthless was the attitude towards him or her. But there was nothing to be done about it; other people really needed that way of asserting power! However, their bullying was not sophisticated: they beat us, spat on us, and wrote humiliating inscriptions on the walls, showing, in general, their innate and idiotic lack of imagination. Thus, we easily anticipated almost all of their mean acts and kinks, with rare exceptions only. You know, when you are warned, it feels like you are protected, so we weren't hurt that much and at times we were even proud of ourselves and of our ability to foresee events.

The following year everybody in the foster home started talking about the significant changes to our country which were known as Perestroika[9]. Nobody knew the meaning of the word and nobody took any interest in it, so what we knew was just rumor, but who actually could we discuss it with, given our situation in that solitary unsightly "cripples and freaks home" run by a corrupt power?

Sprinter had successfully graduated from a ten-year school and enrolled at a technical school for weaving; she was as proud of herself as if she had won a gold medal in the Olympic Games. Her parting ceremony was very peculiar. During the lunch Wash'em'Clean hastily approached her table with his usual hobbling gait, followed by Seamstress, Ragbag and Snot. Lately, they had taken to hanging out together.

"Ah-are you l-leaving us, you limped th-thing?" Wash'em'Clean

---

9   Perestroika – general name of reforms and new ideology of the Soviet management used to designate great changes in the economic and political structure of the USSR. Reforms were developed by the order of Yu. V. Andropov, the Secretary General of the Central Committee of the Communist Party of the Soviet Union, and initiated by M. S. Gorbachev in 1985. Perestroika is considered to have started in April, 1985.

uttered, licking his cracked lips. He had a strange speech impediment; it was neither mumbling nor stammering, more a queer combination of the two. Sprinter nodded complacently.

"I guess, we will never s-see you again out-t-side the place?"

"I don't think so," she said, and, as she had finished her portion of mashed potatoes, moved her plate aside.

"W-well, g-go to h-hell then!"

Like a huge spider hanging over the table, he bent over and spat in her tea, with relish. Everybody who was present in the dining-room, including cooks and caregivers, went deadly silent. One by one, other participants of the "procession" came up to Sprinter's table and also spat in her glass in turn. The most abundant spit was Snot's; she was the last one and had probably been accumulating saliva for a long time.

It always turns out this way: at first people idolize you, swear to be your faithful friend forever, and then they spit in your tea, and on your soul, too.

Sprinter was obviously at a loss. Having raised her shoulders high and biting her lower lip, she trembled all over, either with indignation or with fear, and could do nothing. We didn't believe our eyes. How could it be that for all this time, all her bold actions were masks to hide ordinary fear and lack of self-confidence? Once the spitting was over, the red-haired Sprinter got up and, not looking at anybody, headed for the exit, accelerating like a real sprinter! We thought we had seen the last of her.

Those days our life didn't seem as ugly as I came to see it afterwards. That's why we didn't even think of how detestable it actually was when Adoter, using the opportunity to be awarded for originality, took us to her countryside house to show us to her friends and relations. Imagining ourselves astronauts looking for life on another planet, we were pleased to perform our new "duties": we served food and drinks to the guests and cleared away dishes, serving as some kind of a gaping-stock. The table in the living room laid with heavy plates was literally groaning, standing firm on its thin legs only by a miracle. There were dishes with crabs and salmon, several plates with black and red caviar, vases with oranges and even a pineapple. But we always looked at sweets only. Our "service", however, didn't last long; soon, the idle curiosity of the guests was replaced by acrimonious irritation arising from our deformity; and the principal "dismissed" us at once. For the rest of our life we remembered this fantastic table which we hadn't had the luck to taste a bit from.

We were already in the last grade when a newcomer appeared in the foster home. He had been accidentally run over by a car, and afterwards got on to the operating table. Despite a series of surgical interventions, he remained paralyzed from the waist down. He wasn't able to attend an ordinary school anymore and could not afford home-schooling either: he had no father, and his mother worked as a cleaner, washed the floors of entrance halls in apartment buildings. Adoter, without thinking twice, nicknamed him Disaster, quite up to her shameless style. We met him in the library for the first time. He was moving in his wheelchair between racks of books, his expression thoughtful. Upon seeing us, he immediately drove to our table and smiled in a lively manner.

"Hi! I have already heard about you." He spoke very straightforwardly as if he had known us all his life. His face was distinguished by large eyes, beautiful in a feminine way; his neck was crossed by a scar, a mark testifying to an attempt at suicide. "My name is Sasha."

"They call us One-Two. And what name did they give you?"

"My name is Sasha for everybody, with no exceptions. I don't respond to nasty monikers. So, let's start once again. My name is Sasha, and you are...?"

"Hope and Faith," we corrected ourselves, not fully understanding the strength bestowed on this person whose health and fate were broken but not his spirit.

"How many pillows do you have on your bed?"

This unexpected question baffled us at once; at least, it sounded very unusual within the walls of a foster home.

"One." We exchanged glances.

"Certainly, I knew it."

"But it would be great to have two," I said regretfully, *suddenly* realizing how full of injustices was our situation.

He nodded knowingly.

"So what is the problem? Are you going to sleep on one pillow for the rest of your life? And think about that disgraceful staff. Their lack of brains is not a serious problem, but they have no conscience either. And why is that old TV standing in the assembly hall when it's broken anyway?" (Actually, the TV had been operable and used to gather a large audience around it in the past.) "And this blistering cold. It is already late November, and the rooms are not heated yet. Are they intentionally tormenting us, in order not to show us any mercy? They'll keep making it worse."

"How old are you?" I parried. "How come you understand everything immediately?"

"Where there's a will, there's a way - to push the limits! He who has eyes will see himself; and also, certainly, there are plenty of books in this place."

He often used the word "certainly", but it did not impair his speech at all and even made it more convincing.

"And, certainly, wherever you go in this foster home, you will surely meet either Petrovna or Ilyinichna; quite a narrow choice," he smiled bitterly. "One'd think that all of them only had one father, or that *somebody* with boundless imagination had gifted them the same patronymics *not* quite accidentally.[10]"

"Petrovna and Ilyinichna; that means there were at least two fathers." You decided to show your wit.

"Unfortunately, it doesn't change our situation; all of them are like peas in a pod."

He always had an opinion on just about anything and everything, often contradicting the general way of thinking, that is if you agree that people think generally.

I had so many questions for him, but didn't have the heart to ask them. Having said goodbye politely, he drove off. For the remainder of the evening I couldn't concentrate on my reading.

He appeared to be right on at least one point, because the frosty weather came. December began with strong frosts that covered the windows with icy patterns. There was virtually no heating on the premises. At classes, everybody, including teachers, sat in their outdoor clothing, and once someone started talking, white velvety steam wallowed from his or her mouth. Hot water was supplied once a week. Washed laundry couldn't get dry. You and I were lucky because we could warm each other; the rest of the residents had a very hard time. Thus, life in the foster home got considerably worse. Not just because of the cold, the bad teachers, the poor food; all that was just a consequence. The actual reason was that no one in the foster home management took responsibility for anything and no one had the slightest wish to change

---

10   Petrovna and Ilyinichna are patronymics, i.e., in Russian, components of a personal name based on the given name of one's father; in this specific case, fathers' names would be Pyotr and Ilya, respectively.

anything, each suffering quietly from his own misfortune. All of them had ceased to resist and were resigned to their pathetic, unfortunate existence, and we had to live among them, all of us except Sasha.

Sasha! So many bittersweet memories of mine are associated with that person. I couldn't imagine anyone standing up for us, not even once, but he did it with admirable regularity, for which he was often scourged. Adoter had been looking for a chance to punish him for quite a while, and one day an opportunity arose. She was walking along the corridor and called him:

"Disaster, you were told to appear before me in my office. Hey, I'm talking to you!" she raised her voice, but not reacting, he continued to move on in his wheelchair.

Marfa Ilyinichna overtook him and, standing in his way, exclaimed indignantly:

"Just look at him! Rules are set for everybody, but he doesn't even bother."

"What shall we do with this non-compliant patient?" Adoter said broodingly. "Our good old *educational methods* don't work with him. I think he should be put in the isolation cell."

"Well, the isolation cell it is, Inga Petrovna," Marfa agreed, timidly nodding her head.

"Then make sure it's done," the principal ordered, turning around and walking off.

"So that's how rules are set up here," Sasha couldn't restrain himself from shouting at her back. "Being oneself is considered a crime!"

Adoter, not even changing her pace, only said: "Five days," and disappeared.

Why are we punished? Why do we accept it? What are we guilty of? Of being disabled, being abandoned, being children, not able to stand up for ourselves? Is that how the rules are set up?

Following his conviction, Sasha never responded to his nickname, for which he was repeatedly sent to the isolation cell. He was given a blanket party, beaten in the presence of other kids, but it didn't change anything; he kept obstinately to his path, holding his own ground. "You can kill me, but *my real name* is going to be inscribed on my tombstone!"

Not being afraid of anybody, not relying on anyone or anything, not applying force, Disaster turned into the most dangerous person in the entire foster home.

"They beat you because they envy you," he told us.

"Do you think anyone can envy *us*?" you asked with mistrust.

"Certainly. Practically everybody here, including me, hasn't got the slightest chance of a full recovery. We, cripples, understand this, and we envy anyone who has the slightest chance of leading a normal life. And you do have one!"

I thought he scoffed at us too, in his own, very sophisticated way, through his own abasement, but this wasn't the case.

"I have read about conjoined twins being separated surgically in the capital city."

And with a friendly smile he subtly stroked each of us on the shoulder. The very thought of separation filled us with excitement.

"But what do we have to do?" I asked agitatedly, trying to grab his sleeve. It seemed he wanted to confuse us intentionally.

"There are two options. The first is to try to send your clinical record to the capital city where some big head of science might just get interested in your case. The second is to go there yourselves."

There it was: the reference point, the thought that instantly changed our life and filled it with hope. Now we had a goal. What we needed to do now was to start moving towards it.

First we went into Pyotr Ilyich's office and patiently allowed him to do a regular check-up. For a full hour he had been humming some vivacious marching tune, but once we started explaining the reason for our visit, he immediately stopped humming and turned sad.

"Whoever told you this would be practicable?" he gloomily looked at us from under his bushy eyebrows. "According to your medical record, and I don't need an X-ray examination to confirm it, you have one liver for two. And which one of you is going to have it, huh? Isn't that an interesting case?" he made a long, painful pause and then continued: "Anyway, it is not a big deal to prepare the necessary papers, but I need permission from the principal. Come on, follow me."

His personal involvement distinguished him from the rest of the personnel. Hastily, as though afraid of being late, he dragged us into the office of the person with the least interest in us.

"Pyotr Ilyich, what you suggest sounds like a terrible experiment, the result of which will be that these girls will die. And who is going to bear the responsibility for that?" Adoter asked rhetorically, her eyes piercing Pyotr Ilyich. "You, perhaps? You who never cared about your wife when she was alive, and what would your daughter say about it?"

"I thought, maybe, you..." he started stammering, and then stopped, twitching his eyebrows.

"No, not me. That is not one of my duties – to subject children to homicide. First, they have to graduate from school, to reach full age, and then we can talk." She finished her speech and glanced around at everybody, as if waiting for a response, then when no one said anything she added, "You remember, last week, I announced the commission coming soon to inspect our institution? Only after their visit will I be able to proceed with other matters."

She was dictatorial, as always. Fine wrinkles outlined her mouth, only this time she didn't eat any sweets.

We were exultant and, of course, confided our joy to Sasha. But, for some reason, he just chillily shrugged his shoulders and didn't say anything.

* * *

Sometimes it seems that my recollections are full of omissions and inaccuracies. Suddenly my memory goes, leaving blank spaces up above. Reality distorts everything but still remains reality. Life resembles a continuous dream.

Several months before our graduation I got a bad fever. I had never experienced anything like it before: there was a splendid, luminous, vivid feeling glowing in my chest. I still can't explain my condition, no, not even today. Ready to hover like a butterfly, full of bubbling energy, I could sing silly tunes, laugh at anything, be forgetful and absent-minded, dreaming of our future separation surgery and even our full recovery. I forced you to follow the same route *he* used to walk on, visit the library more seldom, and have long walks in the garden. You couldn't keep ignoring the way I felt, and one day you poured out your "truth" to me; it hit me like a bucket of cold water:

"You have fallen in love, Faith. Very strange choice, I must say, for he's just a cripple. So what are you going to do now?"

"I have not fallen in love!" I replied indignantly, offended by your words because they were my very own thoughts. "And how can you call him a cripple when he can do fifteen press-ups in a row?"

"Nevertheless, you've understood who I'm talking about," you grinned. It was true, I couldn't object.

"I am lost," popped out of me. "What shall I do?"

"You're funny; now you are asking me the same question. Keep it to yourself, hide your feelings, and watch from the sidelines. You know everything pretty well: you have no chance. And even if you had, what would you do with the cripple? Don't even think of it."

You killed me with your words. I could understand and agree with you in my mind, but my heart had a will of its own. I burst into tears; you watched dispassionately, and then said in a conciliatory tone:

"Well, maybe, we will be lucky and find good doctors; they will study our case and separate us in no time at all. You will come back here on *two* legs, confess your feelings to Sasha, and the two of you will move far, far away from here."

Thank you, sister, and thank you a thousand times more. Despite being a realist, you never deprived me of the ultimate hope.

In the winter, when the cold got *really* cold, mischief imprisoned the foster home – a severe flu epidemic came. All the children who had parents were promptly sent home. But some of them got sick so badly that their parents couldn't manage to provide them with proper treatment and the kids were brought back to the foster home. The school was temporarily closed. Pyotr Ilyich treated us for some time, but soon got ill himself. Practically all personnel ceased to show up for work, excusing themselves, being afraid of catching flu. Only Adoter sat solemnly in her unheated office, wearing a long fur coat, like the Snow Queen, and seemed absolutely immune to every kind of germ.

I was the first to get sick and soon infected you. We coughed, sneezed, dripping with snot, but at least we were able to walk; the others couldn't even get up. The worst was our bed neighbor Half-Jane, who for several days couldn't even lift her head up off the pillow and complained of nausea and stomach aches. She looked awful: pale, drawn face, clotted hair. Looking at her was breaking my heart. We forced ourselves to go to the medical unit for help, but there was nobody in there. Illness had turned the foster home into an empty beehive. In the corridor we accidentally bumped into the only living soul around, a duty therapist who was about to leave. Having explained the situation, we only just managed to drag her into the room. She examined Half-Jane and concluded:

"It's an ordinary cold. Now I'll give you an injection, and by Monday you're going to be all right."

She gave Half-Jane a shot, kindly patted her on the cheek and left till Monday. Half-Jane fell asleep but after a while she woke up and continued complaining of severe pain, then became silent again; occasionally, we could hear her subdued sobbing. However, later, she started howling with a vengeance; obviously, the attack had started again. Despite their own sickness, girls complained and got angry with her when she made a loud, drawling groan. By the evening her groans deepened and became non-human, and we went to call for help again. We didn't find anybody in the medical unit, so we went to the reception desk in the hopes of finding someone. The concierge, in wonderful, robust, good health, sat at the reception desk knitting a sock. You said hello and tried to explain everything, but the old woman pretended not to understand anything and kept on knitting. You couldn't restrain yourself and demanded that she let you use the phone.

"Give me Adoter's phone number."

"I shouldn't."

"It's urgent. One girl feels really bad."

"I shouldn't," the old woman repeated stubbornly. "What's on your mind? Go back to your room!"

"We won't leave. Let us make the call," you insisted.

But the concierge only closed the window in our faces and turned off the light.

We stood thinking for a while; you still felt feverish; we had to return to the room. Half-Jane was sleeping and it seemed that the most terrible time had already passed. We sighed with relief but later she started moaning again, asking for a bedpan several times, tossing and turning in the bed; even half-asleep I heard her crying, and for the first time I felt a strong compassion for a stranger. My heart fell when I looked at her, and I reproached myself for not being able to help her.

"My God, I can't bear it. She's keeping everybody awake!" Godly Girl yelled, getting out of the bed. "I'm going to the guys' room to ask for a pill for her so that she will shut up."

"You'd do better to bring her some poison," Snot hissed.

On her return Godly Girl declared:

"The men's room is half empty; there are only the sick ones, all of them bed-ridden."

"Is Sasha there?" I asked, trying to make it sound casual.

"Disaster," you specified unconcernedly.

"I don't know, it was dark there," Godly Girl muttered and went to bed again.

And Half-Jane lay in agony, alone, till dawn, never stopping sobbing and tossing her head on the bed. At daybreak she woke everybody up with loud vomiting. After spitting hard, she fell back on her pillow, and I, being half asleep, could hear her quiet, meek voice. All the others in the room strained their ears to hear her words:

"All of us are lumped together here like kittens in a bag; and no matter how hard you kick or scratch, it's all in vain, nobody's going to hear you," she croaked and, apparently, laughed. "This is my last year in this damned hole," (ours too!), "and I won't get into a technical school; they'll send me to some bloody nursing home. I am going to lie there, young, among the old shit, and decay alive. But I don't want, oh dear, I don't want to die. *I don't want to!*"

She started waving her hands like an insane person, and then she covered her face with a pillow.

Nobody felt better. Our stomachs ached, our heads were splitting, our legs seemed to be made of raw iron, our arms did not obey. But we put ourselves together to get up, shuffled off to the empty dining room and brought her back some breakfast. She only had tea, and then threw up again. Holding on to her stomach, she muttered something deliriously, from time to time howling from the pain. We dared approach her and I touched her forehead which turned out to be very hot; she evidently had a fever. There was nothing for it but to go to the guys' room for advice. Inside we found only several sick boys on their beds; Sasha was among them. Despite shivering with fever, he was sitting on the edge of his bed and reading a book; at the sight of us he brightened up. As for myself, I just can't describe the joy I felt at seeing him; I had missed him so much. Without wasting time, you took the initiative and started telling him how bad Half-Jane's condition was and how we had tried to seek help but found only locked doors. I stood quietly by and almost couldn't hear anything, just gazed about. Your voice reached me as though from far away, but before my eyes was only *him*; I couldn't take notice of anyone else in the room, even though I looked at everyone except him.

"It seems like poisoning," Sasha said. "And it is not surprising at all. Lately we have been fed like cattle."

"What shall we do?" you asked.

"About her? What can we do? We have to call an ambulance, or Inga Petrovna."

He even called Adoter Inga Petrovna. He got into his wheelchair and accompanied us on our search. The window at the reception desk was locked; clearly, we were late; nobody seemed to care. We went round the entire foster home but did not meet any of the employees. Only in the dining room did we manage to find some spark of life in the shape of the rectangular-bodied cook. Sasha tried to explain the danger Half-Jane was in, but the cook muttered something about the borsch she was cooking which allegedly she had to keep an eye on all the time, and she quickly left for the kitchen.

When we came back to our room, we found Half-Jane delirious, all wet; she had already stopped groaning. She was pale and her eyes were wan like those of a rotten fish. I had never seen anything like it before. Her breath was fast and irregular, but it sometimes stopped as if she were constraining herself and did not want to disturb anybody; or maybe that was her way of fighting the pain. Godly Girl, red as a crawfish, put a wet towel on her glowing forehead and lamented with fear. Exhausted, we dropped on to our bed and fell asleep at once. Sasha returned to his room. It was completely dark outside when I heard a deafening crack, resembling radio interference rather than an indistinct whisper. I woke you up and, having found our shoes by touch in the dimly lit room, we approached Half-Jane's bed. She seemed to be completely out of her senses, her pupils were enlarged, her face has drawn. For a while she opened her mouth but didn't make a sound, putting her gray tongue out, then with force she grabbed hold of the sheets as someone falling over a precipice might grab hold of bushes, turned her head to one side, and, having made her last gasp, quietened down.

I can only vaguely remember what happened afterwards; I was probably crying or sleeping. In the morning I saw Sasha who took a lively interest in recent events, then Marfa Ilyinichna's scared face replaced his, and at last, Adoter appeared, accompanied by the new head physician. He examined Half-Jane with unspeakable disgust and announced:

"The death occurred somewhere between three and four o'clock in the morning."

"A merciful release," Marfa said under her breath.

"The autopsy will show the reason," the physician concluded loftily.

"Reason!" I nearly cried. "What the hell! She died of human indifference. She died right in front of our eyes."

Her body lay in the room till evening, and then they put her on a filthy blanket and carried her away to the basement. She was buried the next morning by our own efforts. After digging a shallow pit in the frozen ground with great difficulty, the boys lowered the body, wrapped up in old sheets, into it. After returning to our room, we went into the bathroom and cried for a long time; cried in turn, as we had agreed to do before this dreadful event. We mourned not only the deceased girl, but also ourselves; it seemed so offensive and terrible that we could appreciate Half-Jane only after she had died.

There was no monument, no cross on her grave – just a tin plate saying "Zinaida Stepanovna Puss". That's when we finally found out Half-Jane's real name.

Disaster

About a week later, several inspectors came to the foster home. Adoter accompanied them every second. First, she showed them the dining room, the gym and the physiotherapy procedure rooms, and then she took them away to the academic building. When they entered our room, everybody stopped talking; Adoter, with a straight face, answered the trickiest questions with ease. We stood by in cowardly silence. It really should be stated that the foster home had been put in order prior to the inspection: doctors showed up for work, the school was open again and everyone was in his or her place. Even the lavatory had been scrubbed clean with chloride lime; however, the heating was still off, its absence blamed on force-majeure circumstances, natural phenomena beyond reasonable control.

A day before the inspection, Adoter had gathered everybody in the assembly hall and, strolling between the rows, repeated how important it was to respect the established standards. Her speech was uneven and at times devoid of any sense whatsoever. Indeed, she seemed unable to understand many of her own statements, but all her declarations could be summarized in the following: Behave quietly, do not complain, do not stand out. This was nothing new; such a slogan had been repeated and re-enforced a thousand times to disabled children spending their unpretentious lives "under the roof of her house".

Everything went well and the examination was already proceeding to its well-greased and predictable end when some inspectors decided to take a look in the men's room. I don't know exactly what happened in there, but after a while they leaped out of it with gray faces; the procession was brought up by a running and very agitated Adoter who was trying to explain something. Apparently she was successful, because we never saw them again.

An unspoken rule was applied in the foster home: never wash your dirty linen in public, and woe betide anyone who did. Sasha tried because he was convinced that he could break the rigid system single-handedly. He told the guests from the capital city about everything that was happening in the home and what he had witnessed himself. It came as a bombshell. By the evening rumors had spread that Disaster's days were numbered and that he wouldn't be let off with incarceration in the isolation cell. I knew trouble waited for him, but I could not imagine its full extent.

The next day we were arranged in rank in the assembly hall once again. There was a strange, hardly describable smile on Adoter's face. If you have ever seen somebody smiling at a funeral, you may have a notion what she looked like. She pointed her finger at Sasha, asked him to "step" forward, and to turn and face everyone.

"Something happened in our foster home yesterday, something unpredictable and gross. A patient in our big and close-knit family disapproves of everything here. He firmly opposes the rules and does not agree with living like everybody else and being content with his lot. He also enjoys grassing to the authorities. Now, I must ask all of you, is there anyone else who feels like this fellow, my critic, your critic, our critic? Please, don't hesitate. Take a step forward. We must know our heroes, and our critics, by sight." And she looked around at everyone very slowly.

That was probably the look the Gorgon used on her victims the first and the last time – clear, cold, stony. There is a type of fear that makes you run away, but the fear we felt at that moment was totally different. We were all petrified, not only in our bones but also in our minds. Afterwards, I kept coming back to that moment, trying to understand why no one had taken a step forward but it was obvious why. We were scared out of our wits. We were weak. We were selfish.

An ominous, almost tangible silence reigned in the hall. Adoter spoke in a whisper, but everybody could hear her quite distinctly:

"Doesn't anyone want to support Alexander? Are all you others happy? Doesn't anyone want to complain about anything?"

Sasha was sitting in his wheelchair with his head down, paying no attention to her words.

"Do you see, Alexander, what I see," Adoter said and haughtily raised her exquisitely shaped eyebrows. "You are all alone, just an upstart who is impossible to please. For your actions you deserve to be publicly shamed and reproved. From now on you are to be ostracized; anyone who starts talking to you will be punished. I will personally supervise any punishment that needs to be administered. Did everyone hear that?"

All the kids nodded in unison; their eyes bent on the ground and hands by their sides.

"Excellent. Now you can all bear witness to how opposition to rules and the established order leads to destruction and personal mishap," she said somewhat loftily, beginning her dreadful conclusion. "Ten days in the isolation cell. And this punishment awaits anyone who dares talk to him," she concluded raising her voice somewhat. "All dismissed!"

In the isolation cell Sasha spent only seven days of his "term". He fell severely ill and was urgently transferred to the hospital room. I was eager to see him again and we paid him a visit as soon as possible. He lay absolutely still, with his face turned towards the wall, and examined spots on its white surface, but once we greeted him, he jumped off his bed like a spring, using his hands only. He was extremely surprised to see us.

"You must not talk to me. Go away; I don't want you to be punished."

We didn't expect to be reproved.

"We've brought you your favorite books," I mumbled for no good reason and put the books on his bedside table. "I am sorry for not supporting you before the principal. And now we don't care if they punish us. You did the right thing and we were being cowards."

"I was extremely foolish. It is too late to change anything; all that is left is regret. I am a fool; I was so high-minded, thinking I could change things with desire and will. Whoever believes those silly books with their ideals, all that lofty nonsense, they're idiots. They believe a total lie. It doesn't happen in real life."

He grabbed a book at random and started tearing pages out of it, scattering them around the room. We impulsively dashed to him and hugged him, but he pushed us away, and shouted:

"Leave me alone, get out, go away!"

It was evident that he had suffered and was suffering immensely. Terrified, we moved back and then broke into a run without looking back. Our hearts were beating madly, we were out of breath, running into our room, and our strength gave out. Should I mention the anguish that crushed me? I sobbed at the top of my voice till I was blue in the face, and you, next to me, seemed to be drowning in depression. I can still see the scene: we are rushing along the corridor and behind us Sasha is tearing the rest of his books. Since then I have realized that he and I could never be together, but why does that dreadful end live on in my memory to be repeated in painful drabness?

A week later, his hands started trembling severely, his face turned pale, his eyes faded, and the top of his left eye twitched. He looked much older; he was withering away.

"He seems to have been poisoned. They must have given him some pills or shots that make him weak-minded," I sobbed, sharing my guess with you. "If they keep doing that, he will soon turn into an idiot."

You nodded in agreement:

"I think we need to talk to him before it's too late."

We found him sitting by the window. This time he was absentmindedly examining the frosty patterns on the windowpane.

"Sasha," I started as calmly as I could, hardly quietening my shiver, "just look at yourself; they are really trying to poison you; you could end up in a bad way!"

"I don't care," he said droopingly, without taking his eyes off the window and weirdly wringing his hands. "They do what they have to do; the system destroys everyone who tries to overturn it. It is a general rule."

"No," I cried, "humiliation and low acts must not become the norm. You ought to fight."

"They will kill you," you interrupted.

"It's OK," he answered and smiled ironically. "I must be grateful to the killing knife for being so sharp."

"But you can't give up just like this," I nearly cried. "You have to live."

"For the sake of what and for whom?" he asked with a kind of furious hopelessness. "Perhaps for the sake of my mother who left me to the mercy of *fate*? I have written her dozens of letters and still get no answer."

"They open all the letters before sending them and, maybe, they did not send yours at all." I tried to help him, grasping at any chance, wanting to motivate him. "They always act this way: push those who are falling. And in the end *I need you*."

Why did I add this? Was it because it was the truth I could not conceal, the truth that always looks for a way out? Or was there something more behind it? Maybe someone's unreason can only be remedied with new unreason? But Sasha wasn't listening...

"Certainly, in my letters I was only saying what a great time I was having here and how good everything was. Could I possibly tell her the truth about what was actually going on here?" he responded with irritation. "Why any opposition, why any change, when nobody cares, just like my own mother who doesn't care about me?"

We spent a little more time with him, but he didn't say anything else, just waited for us to go away.

Why didn't I fight for him? Can my apathy be called treachery? What would Sasha have done if he was me? Would he have neglected his own personal safety? Would he have turned away or fought? I think I know the answer. It's obvious. But, for now, I realized Sasha was flying so high above us that when he did fall, he fell below everybody else. Seemingly a paradox, but true. To be precise, he was merely knocked down. And we, none of us, did anything to protect or support him. With everybody's silent acquiescence, the best were eliminated in order to let the worst carry on. We were responsible for our own decay. We were the worst. That is how I saw it.

You usually lose your dearest people long before their deaths. For three more long weeks he stirred the minds of in the residents of the foster home because everybody noticed the changes in his personality, but at the beginning of March, Sasha got transferred to a mental home. As a strange coincidence, from that day the radio station stopped broadcasting the national anthem which accompanied the awakening of a great nation every morning. But almost no one noticed it, and the foster home continued living its usual, meaningless life. Sasha's mother had never come once to visit him.

Is there an alarm clock to wake one's conscience? And who knows the exact time when it is going to go off? Sometimes a person planning to commit a crime gets caught up in the passion of the deed, but afterwards, he or she can't bear the pangs of conscience. Death follows.

A week later Adoter got sick, and when she returned to her workplace she looked much more aged. The changes were striking: haggard face, streaks of gray in her hair, and deeper and more visible wrinkles between her eyebrows. But her gait had changed most of all; now she was walking heavily and tiredly, giving the impression that she had an enormous load on her shoulders. Unwillingly, she started resembling the patients in her own foster home like two hands on the same body which resemble each other.

* * *

The last month of the academic year was approaching; the atmosphere grew tenser and tenser with each day. Adoter seemed to rust through and through, and then she lost all her former dexterity at problem solving. Nervous and increasingly revengeful, she now made the most out of the most minor misconduct, imagining dissent even when there was absolutely no sign of it. The isolation cell filled up!

Meanwhile, we were finishing our studies. I had no idea what would happen to us after graduation, where fate would toss us, but, in truth, I didn't care. Deprived of the person I loved, I had lost interest in life. I grieved all the time but was also ashamed of my own grief.

I remember how immensely supportive you were at that time, and I am still very grateful to you. At first I thought that you were simply pursuing your own goals to survive at any cost; not able to feel the entirety of another person's loss, you were just guided by life instincts because if I suffer, you suffer too, but it was only later that I understood that performing the role of an elder sister, catering and caring for me, was a real pleasure to you. You lent me your shoulder to cry on, a crutch to a cripple, and you believed that by helping me you could find yourself. It was only after this incident with Sasha that you and I got as close as only two conjoined people can get. Since then I have always felt we are one person with two souls.

We eventually managed to solicit the new head physician to pass our clinical record on to Inga Petrovna for her approval. The day before I had a nightmare that began with a message of hope but ended horribly. We reached the capital city, found competent and decent doctors who successfully separated us. And, of course, having gained independent life at last, we rejoiced like children; it seemed that life was smiling on us. But the happiness didn't last long. I woke up one morning to find our bodies joined again. In panic, I tried to tear myself away or at least to move, but I wasn't able to. Then I turned my head to the right, but instead of you I unexpectedly found Adoter;

now she was connected to me! Gosh, at that very moment I definitely realized the full horror of our situation, that we will never be able to leave ourselves and the home, that we are trapped forever and forever. I woke up in a cold sweat and found you peacefully sniffing beside me.

Right after breakfast we went to the principal's office. The moment of truth had arrived. We knocked several times, went in and saw Adoter pretentiously lying back in a spacious armchair. Her usual irritable mood had been replaced by sleepiness and boredom, but once you started on the subject of our surgery, Adoter's face twitched and livened up, distorting itself into a grimace of laughter. Only her eyes remained serious.

"Well, well, just look at you! What nonsense! And which head of this two-headed lizard came up with such a remarkable idea? So, it is not enough for you to live at the expense of the public but you also want and believe experiments should be performed on you. Would you like to be normal like everybody else?" She cleared her throat several times; her voice was piercing and penetrating. "The looking glass is not to blame if your face is plain. The world is not going to be any better off after your separation. I have seen many ugly people in my life; they have all had to live with their ugliness. Always has been like this, always will be."

We thought we were used to her insults, but she always seemed able to invent new and ever more exquisite ways of hurting and insulting. She looked at us with indignation and abhorrence as if we were annoying insects, and relished our suffering, trampling on the remains of our frail dignity, not only ours, but hers, too.

"I am not going to send your documents to anybody. You have to accept things as they are. You will stay here as long as the stars stay above you! And *that* is final!"

Leisurely, almost unwillingly, she opened a drawer, took out a folder, extracted the papers from it, arranged them into three equal piles and slowly started tearing.

Pieces of paper were flying all over the office as if winter and cold were back again with a vengeance. For some fraction of a second I realized with inevitable clarity that our clinical records were in shreds and that the record of our life was soaring in the air and settling on the floor where it couldn't exist anymore.

"That's it," Adoter summed up; her eyes were filled with genuine tears, her lips, slightly quivering, expressed a triumphant smile, from time to time changing to a deep sadness. "You have never existed. There is only the counting: One-Two, one, two. And now get out of here and don't forget to close the door behind you."

We didn't have any strength left to resist or talk or argue. Everything ended up crumbled, dead, far away. Our strength existed merely to sustain silence and emptiness. We were leaving when suddenly you found the force to turn back. You said quietly, very distinctly:

"Actually, Inga, Adolf's daughter, you are sitting in this cage too, together with us; and apparently it can never end."

We had no doubt that we were going to be punished, sent to the isolation cell or maybe even worse, to the funny farm; we were waiting for her reprisal, but it never came. I believe that was the last and the most artful revenge of all. The expectation of something inevitable happening which would be painful and long-lasting. We were permanently on alert and actually already trapped inside the walls of the nut house. Day by day our humiliation, the insults, and our anguish were repeated as in an infinite depressive dream. There were two choices: to resign ourselves and continue living in fear and anxiety or to fight. Without thinking twice, we chose the latter, and kept our heads down, cunningly and scrupulously watching everyone's movements, over long months.

Another winter came. Slabs of the fencing surrounding the foster home moved apart, forming a narrow aperture with width enough for a human body to squeeze through. A few inmates occasionally crept out, ran to the neighboring village to procure vodka or cigarettes and then ran back. We needed to find out if we would be able to squeeze through a crack in that fencing easily, but how could we do so? The doors of the building were diligently locked at night and we saw no opportunity of getting near the fencing. Guys got out of the building through a second-floor window, sliding down on sheets tied together; that was the only verified method. But it didn't suit us at all; it's hard to imagine conjoined twins going down a rag rope. Daytime, we carefully searched through the whole yard looking for a suitable place to hide, but without success. The entire territory was plainly visible, and night watchmen, having closed all the doors of the buildings, inspected it twice a night. We became discouraged, ready to surrender, but then a great idea dawned on you, a real brainwave.

"We will hide in the *isolation cell*. We will get the keys at the reception desk and spend all day there, locked up within. At night we'll get out, reach the fencing, and we'll be free!"

Of course I realized that we had to commit another theft and endure another stay in the isolation cell, this time one dictated to by our own initiative, but we didn't have a choice. Perhaps not everything bad is in fact bad.

All spring and almost all summer we waited for the isolation cell to become vacant. In early September, when Adoter took a vacation, our time came. We had to wash clothes for skinny

Snot through the whole, sad summer. In return she would steal the cherished keys when the right time came. When everything was ready we locked ourselves inside the "penal institution" that had become loathsome to us, and we lay low till the night came.

Only in movies does the course of events fly fast with everything changing from bad to good and ending best. Real life is quite different. The time we spent in that isolation cell dragged on indefinitely; it seemed we were sitting there forever and were going to leave those lifeless walls in our dotage. If only reality were similar to movie-reality, how easy life would be!

We watched day changing to night through the rusted keyhole. After waiting for several hours, we got out with relief. It was cool outside, and you suggested taking an old blanket – another theft! Like thieves making a cautious escape, we hid behind buildings and slowly got to the engineering unit of the foster home. There, behind a network of pipes, was a narrow opening in the fence. A chilling discovery… there seemed no way through, but we managed it! After getting out, we started our journey down the nearest footpath with great determination, a starless sky lighting our poor progress, conjoined twins, making a lucky escape.

Undefeated War

Evening fog was slowly wrapping itself around the wood; the air turned blue and dense. In the dim light of the moon we looked like two identical black shadows. The stately wood seemed to be both a monster and a savior at the same time. A river murmured somewhere far away. Several times we stumbled and fell down, clinging to the roots of the trees, damp from dew.

"We are far enough away," you said quietly as if afraid that you might be heard. "We need to take a rest. Let's get some sleep – in turns: first you, then me. It's safer that way."

We spent our first restless night under an old wide-branching oak. You laid your head on my shoulder and fell asleep right away... and woke up in the morning feeling refreshed, happy and full of energy. It started drizzling, but the leaves covered us from moisture and we didn't get too wet.

"It seemed as if I fell into a deep well," you tried to explain, scratching your head. "Come on, let's go."

Having wrapped the humid blanket around ourselves, we stepped back out onto the footpath and moved on. Of course, I didn't know where the road went; as always, you had a plan which you, however, didn't share with me. It was getting more and more difficult to go on: the rain had washed away the footpath, mud squelched under our feet and seemed to be about to swamp us; the blanket got wet and heavy. Suddenly it came into our minds that we had a couple of chunks of gray bread from the dining room in our pockets, so we stopped under a tree and hastily ate the supplies that were stuck together from the moisture. The rain began to stop. Soon we came across a local village, probably the one that served as a source of bevy, cigarettes and inspiration for our "colleagues" from the foster home.

"Let's go in and ask for some food or milk," I suggested.

"We can't, they may recognize us. Look at us! Ridiculous and far too noticeable. We just don't blend into the village crowd."

Disappointed, I shrugged my shoulders like an anti-Atlas, and we trudged on further. Unexpectedly, as if from under the earth, in the middle of a footpath, there appeared an old woman. She stood still, leaning on a stick; her lips were moving silently.

"What's wrong with her? Is she blind or mad?" you said almost indignantly.

"She's definitely not deaf," I answered in a whisper. "Let's go our way."

Carefully, on tiptoe, we made our way on. Glancing at the woman, I noticed sadness in her heavily aged eyes which were fixed on the distance. Having walked on a little, we saw an old house whose windows evoked shrill melancholy and hopelessness. Here and there the fence beveled, the roof moved apart, a broken lock hung on the open wicket gate. It was getting dark. The rain that had stopped some time ago started once more with a vengeance.

"Let's knock and say we are lost," you said.

"Whatever you do, I'll do too," I agreed immediately. "I'm absolutely shattered."

Having knocked on the door and on the windows, we stood motionless under the canopy – hunched, tired, trying to cover ourselves from the rain – with no success at all. There was only deaf silence in reply. We heard hens cackling somewhere, and noticed a sad cat lying under the bench. Then, emboldened by the absence of the owners, we went up to a shed and walked inside. The hay was crisp under our feet; we saw a pitchfork, empty baskets, scoops and a cartwheel hanging on the walls. Our feet were humming with fatigue, our backs ached.

"It's late; there's no one in the house. Let's wait here till morning," you suggested.

We took off the wet blanket and hung it on a nail to dry, near a pitchfork, then we made up a sort of bed in the hay, took off our shoes and lay down, hugging each other. You shivered with cold and I suffered from the stuffy air; my feet hurt strangely as if I were still walking on a twisty road. For a long time our hunger and fatigue kept us awake. We had to get up and then lie face down. It helped, and we finally managed to fall asleep.

I woke up with the dreadful feeling that someone else was in the shed. Having opened my eyes, I saw the old woman we had met in the wood. She was sitting silently in front of us, deep in thought, and looking at us almost without blinking. I woke you up at once.

"We're caught."

Though I tried to speak quietly, every word was audible. For a minute we all looked at each other: we were confused, and she was pensive. It was paralyzing and made me feel desperate and hopeless.

"Don't be afraid of me. Are you hungry?" she asked kindly, but that didn't stop her scaring me. "Come into the house."

"We are not afraid at all," you announced boldly.

"Well, then, come with me." The old woman slowly rose from the upside-down bucket on which she had been sitting and went towards the house.

"I'm not going to bite you, sweeties," she added in a tone which was meant to encourage us. "Come, come, the meal is getting cold."

"We're coming," you answered resolutely.

"Do you think she noticed our *problem*?" I mumbled while we were trudging through the yard.

"It doesn't matter anymore. We'll have our meal, then ask the way to the nearest station and leave."

The landlady was waiting for us at the door of the old house and invited us in with a gesture. We went in and saw a long corridor with several doors, three on the left and one on the right; there was a bed with curtains hanging over it at the end of the corridor. The old woman opened the first door on the left, and we entered a large kitchen with a big Russian stove and a stove bench, a table with a colorful cloth and a small cauldron on it with tasty smelling food and three empty plates. We sat down on two chairs with warped backs tightly tied together with a rope – obviously, the landlady had taken care of everything beforehand – and she put freshly-baked bread, just out of the stove, on the table. Here and there we could see household items; everything seemed so homely and familiar, as if this was home after long wandering.

"You look very hungry; you're so thin. Help yourselves."

We instinctively muffled ourselves up in the blanket which was still wet because we believed it protected us from unwanted questions. Bread was sliced and plates filled up with hot soup. The landlady sat down opposite us and gave us spoons. Without saying a word, we dug into our food, not even tasting it; after two helpings we were intoxicated with satiety.

Despite her advanced age, the old lady resembled Adoter in some ways. The likeness was so striking, as if she were her mother, but her eyes were absolutely different, sad and thoughtful, and simplicity of character was in her movements and in her voice. Having finished her own meal, she got up, putting her hand on her sore lower back, and told us to follow her. Going back into the corridor, we entered the third door on the left and saw a tiny bedroom with a disproportionately large bed occupying two thirds of the room.

"Here is your bed. Perhaps it's not very comfortable in the shed."

She said goodnight and left. I couldn't make heads or tails of what was happening. Could reality be so chaste and beautiful? This bed with two pillows instead of one, a warm, soft blanket – isn't it a dream? You quickly fell asleep but I restlessly listened to the surrounding sounds, and couldn't decide if I should be afraid or happy. Eventually, fatigue overcame fear and I fell into a deep sleep.

We were woken by a rooster's crow. The sun was shining brightly behind the window and nothing reminded us of yesterday's rain. Having got out of bed, we looked for our blanket for a long while, feeling physiologically dependent on it.

"That granny must have filched it," you said with irritation. "I wonder what she is going to do with it."

"Somehow I doubt that," I mumbled to myself. "What shall we do?"

"She took ours, and we will take hers," you responded quite belligerently.

"Wait!" I protested. The mere thought of another theft drove me crazy. I couldn't contemplate stealing a blanket from such a kind old woman. "Maybe it's not worth it? No blanket – no problems. She will know it is us."

"Yeah," you agreed. "Enough's enough. Come on; let's look for a toilet and a wash basin."

Having left the bedroom, we resumed exploring the house in the light of day. Our attention was drawn to a long corridor connecting the entrance door and other rooms. We could see colored, handmade, patchwork carpets, and beyond, walls covered with yellowish patterned wallpaper interspersed with newspapers hanging like unkempt rags. Behind the middle door on the left we found a spacious drawing room. There was an old sideboard, a rocking chair, a chest, a dresser with a small radio, and a couch. The most memorable items were an abundance of black-and-white photos on the walls and a big cuckoo clock. The only door on the opposite side led to a lavatory attached to a hen house. The most astonishing discovery was the total absence of mirrors, even small ones. We couldn't find any, neither in the bedroom, nor in the bathroom, as if a newly deceased person were in the house.

The kitchen table was laid with bread and boiled potatoes, over which was sprinkled fresh dill; the landlady appeared to have gone out. Confused, we also went out, into the yard where we found our blanket drying on a rope together with other laundry. The old lady, holding two wooden billets in her hands, came out of the shed towards us.

"Have you had your breakfast? I left some food for you."

"We didn't know if it was made for us," I answered.

The old woman looked us over from head to foot again; her gaze gave me that familiar, uncomfortable feeling. Some people's appearances make good impressions on others, but not ours; we have always felt uncomfortable and guilty.

"Here's what," you said, breezily, "we need to make our way to the nearest town."

"You're so thin," the old woman observed, nodding the while and then shaking her head. "Have you got any money?

Let's go into the house first and you will tell me your story," she offered.

Having seated us at the table, Rosa Ivanovna – that was the old woman's name – started firing up a samovar, darkened with soot. She poured tea into three large cups, sat down opposite us and started talking again.

"What are your names, sweethearts?"

"I'm Faith and she is Hope," I said with a tone of pride, believing in the great importance of our names.

"Good ones," she nodded slightly.

And only here, in the kitchen, eating fresh bread with boiled potatoes, I finally realized: our old life with the humiliating nicknames had come to an end. We had abandoned it *forever*, left it in the foster home, exchanged it for an old blanket and our freedom. Caught up in these thoughts, I started examining Rosa Ivanovna and by chance noticed that her teeth were disproportionately big and made of iron. I guess my surprise was unwittingly expressed on my face because the landlady started laughing quietly:

"Don't make that face, honey; they really are iron. On the other hand, they're so hard that I could crack nuts with them. I lost my own long ago. Well, eat. Don't be shy. I know all about hunger."

"Did you live in an orphanage?" I asked naively.

"No, why would you think that? I have been in a great variety of places throughout my life, but I never happened to live in an orphanage. I grew up in a normal family; my best memories go back to those days. I went to school with a black, leather schoolbag; I would never forget that bag. My dad made it for me. He was a shoemaker and crafted boots for the entire town. Mummy was teaching music at a school. She played the violin and taught me how to tweedle, too. I can't express what a beauty she was. As soon as she went out of the house, all the men around her fainted with delight." At first she spoke rather incoherently. Her mind seemed to be wandering, but gradually she organized her thoughts and went on: "My childhood was everyone's envy in every respect, if you understand what I mean. No one could foresee what I would go through later on."

"And what did you go through?" You had stopped chewing and you asked her, direct.

"The War[11]," the old woman said in a shattered voice. "The Germans came and occupied the city, seized power; our house was turned into a heap of ruins. Everything dear to me was wiped out in a moment. Hunger overcame the whole country; people grew blind from crying, weakened by pain and despair; children were dying in bunches. After some months my family was called to the commander's office and informed that we were in for a new work regime in a new town; they sent us immediately to the station where the train was waiting for us. Everything was over, but we kept rejoicing, simple-mindedly, because we were still alive."

"And what happened next?" I was fascinated by her story. "What came after?"

"By a kind of miracle, I managed to survive that journey. Heartbreaking groans split the air. People messed their clothes, choking from the stench of excrement; body and bones were almost breaking from fatigue and pain. Finally, they brought us to Poland. I found it out a while after. Some people died on the way. They were the lucky ones. We were dropped off at a closed transit point where they promptly

---

11   This refers to World War II (lasting from September 1, 1939 till September 2, 1945), the war between the two global military and political coalitions which became the largest armed conflict in the history of mankind.

sorted us out: the old, the sick, children to one side, those capable of working on the other. Dad and Mummy stood about ten meters from me, and I tried to make sure I kept them in sight. Meanwhile they took dead bodies out of the train; I saw many similar pictures later on. Then they drove up another train and loaded people back on. My parents happened to be in the front rows, so they got on immediately and I waited my turn. It never came. I was simply left on the platform. The train started off and I didn't even have the chance to say goodbye to them. So there I was, all alone."

Her voice began to tremble and she turned her face away so that we couldn't see her crying. After calming down, she finished her tea, poured herself another cup and continued:

"They sent me to a German concentration camp where I did cleaning during the day and helped to carry corpses away at night. I have seen so many dead people with crippled bodies, sometimes ugly and deformed in a way that you could never recognize them; I will never be able to forget it. I also happened to see ones like you – conjoined, or, maybe, stitched together on purpose. In fact, those scientist-monsters experimented on living people."

We listened to her with bated breath.

"At the end of the war everyone who had survived was released by the Soviet troops. "Here, at last, is my long-anticipated happiness!" I thought. "I will finally return home, find my parents and continue studying". Who would have known they would declare me public enemy number one in my own country! But that is what they did. After winning the most oppressive war in history, people *continued to be at war with each other*. For several months, they interrogated me, threatened me, starved me, didn't allow me to sleep. I couldn't stand it and I signed their filthy document that was just a piece of horrible slander. I spent ten inconsolable years in the Soviet camps to complete my time. That's where I met my husband, a con[12], too. Without him I wouldn't be sitting here right now. After our release, instead of mixing with people, we decided to keep away from them. We lived in poverty and seclusion and had no children. Soon my husband started drinking. However, he never beat me. We lived in harmony – and after thirteen years of living together in the wild he went missing. I made inquiries, appealed to militia, went to a mortuary for body identification several times, but all in vain. He just disappeared into thin air. And again, I remained all alone with my memories. So, you know what?" Rosa Ivanovna said, "you can stay with me," and a soft smile lit up her face chopped up with wrinkles. "My house is not so big, but there's room enough for the three of us."

Remembering our soft bed with two pillows, I nearly started sobbing. You hadn't planned for a delay. But, to my great surprise, you agreed without hesitation. I didn't know how to thank you. For the first time in my life I realized how it feels to be truly happy.

Every morning, we rose at the earliest cock crow, had our breakfast, and then helped our granny-host do the work around the house though she never asked us to. After lunch we went into the woods where we wandered along familiar footpaths, always far away from the village. But once it started to get dark we grew sad as if our dream sank below the horizon alongside the sun.

---

12   Convict slang - the person subjected to arrest as a restraint measure; the person deprived of freedom under the court verdict and serving the sentence in a special establishment - colony, pretrial detention center, prison, etc.

I read a lot of books which I found in the house. While I was swallowing stories and novels, turning over dust-laden pages, you grew fretful and bored like the master's cat with nothing to do, satiated with benevolence.

There was always plenty of food at Rosa Ivanovna's house. She used to stock up with flour and oil. She was growing all kinds of vegetables and fruit, greens and berries, on her vegetable plot, and her small cellar was always packed to the hilt with various pickles and marinated goods. She never threw out stale bread: part of it she crumbed up for her hens and the rest she used for making rusks which we then had with tea and jam. Her wardrobe comprised three identical dresses and some old shawls. Four pairs of felt boots stood in a corner – every rag, every piece of cloth was useful. She adored speaking about people, their lives, their sufferings, about what everyone has to face. We heard a lot of surprising and often frightening stories from her. Rosa Ivanovna firmly declared that there was going to be another war and lived depressed by her expectation. She believed that the thirst for domination and the thirst for extermination overcame everything.

"I am lucky to have no children," she said once. "God didn't let it happen! And, after all, what would I tell them? About Satan or about our great leaders whose achievements we must be proud of; repeating the lie that everyone is forced to believe in? But how could I lie to my own children? I wouldn't be able to do it; I would tell them the truth – that our leaders are inhuman and their deeds conceal numerous crimes against our nation. And then my children would have to live with the endless fear that their lives were in danger, permanently looking around and straining their ears, telling the truth only in whispers, and, behind closed doors, pretending, lying, wriggling like their parents. And what a life it would be. Eventually, not able to understand what truth is and what lies are, they would opt for the tried and tested method, that is, they would grass to the authorities and live their lives happily ever after. This would be a proven way to take part in the destruction of the world as a whole. So, thank you, God, for not letting it happen."

She dreamt that after her death she would go to some mythical country – for victims of political repression, those gunned down, the fallen, to a superpower inhabited not by parasitic deceivers and cowards, but by real heroes, talented and courageous men and women. I think the reason for her saying this was fear and despair, because no one could truly believe in those kinds of things, right?!

After twenty long and lonely years from when her husband disappeared, Rosa Ivanovna still continued to wait for him, believing he would come back to her one day. Every week she went to the station, and we sometimes accompanied her, wrapped in a blanket, and stood with her on the platform, watching a train, any train, coming. I remember those days. I admired her for her strong, all-consuming, obsessional love; I thought that was the way real love should be. Hardly had the train pulled in before she was beside the first carriage, or else she stopped halfway, probably realizing the futility of her actions. She turned around and slowly trudged away, glancing into the face of every elderly man who had stepped down on to the platform. At that moment, her eyes expressed a strange, unnatural indifference which struck deep in my soul. Now I understand. Behind all those actions was ordinary habit, not love; she was afraid of meeting him, of changing her life of isolation and near death. She had nothing to do, just wait for something and worry about it. Her dismal habit gave her security.

One day, at the end of November, against all our expectations Rosa Ivanovna ordered us to go to the shed and not to stick our heads out of it until she called us. She had a visitor who brought her groceries from the village. While he was unloading the goods we languished in the shed and speculated on *the isolation cell* that had forced its way into our life again; we were condemned to sit *there* for misconduct which we had never been involved in. It seemed like nothing had changed in our life except the scenery; the essence had stayed the same.

"It is time for us to leave; our visit has lasted too long," you said in a low voice, and your eyes sparkled either from tears or from indignation. "If we have started something, well, we are obliged to finish it."

Arguing made no sense; hiding was intolerable. And even if I had known then the price of our operation, our separation, I would still have agreed to this, our second "escape". I perfectly understood how important it was, not only for you, but for both of us; it was worth the risk. The good thing this time was we were able to tell Rosa Ivanovna of our plans.

So, when the old lady heard us out, she looked at us as if she was fated to bury us with her own hands. She sighed a few times, made a helpless gesture but didn't take the liberty of discouraging us, only grunted in conclusion. For two days she made preparations for our journey, muttering to herself the while. As for me, I was happy to have the opportunity to stay for a little bit more, deeply regretting leaving this soft and cozy life which we were never going to live any more.

Rosa Ivanovna found everything we needed: two pairs of felt boots, sweaters, two quilted jackets and woolen shawls. After finishing finding us clothes, she rummaged in the dresser and took out ten red banknotes[13] from under the old, yellowish

---

13   A 10 ruble banknote is referred to here. The average salary in the USSR in the described period equaled to 200 rubles, or 345 US dollars at the

newspapers. She handed them over to us, just letting slip quietly:

"You can repay me when you get the chance to."

"Thank you, we will repay the loan for sure." Saying this, I sincerely believed in my promise, and the granny pretended to believe in it too, though she knew she was looking at us for the last time.

The next day she handed us the bag loaded with food, and our old blanket.

The way to the nearest settlement with a railway station lay through the wood, and the granny volunteered to help us through. On the way she mentioned the difficulties we would have to face and advised us to close our eyes if ever we were scared. It sounded a little childish; and in my mind I dismissed the idea, not understanding how valuable her advice would turn out to be. Reaching the middle of the wood, Rosa Ivanovna stopped abruptly as if coming to an invisible wall.

"From here on you go by yourselves. Alone, forever alone." She spoke loudly, then turned around and walked away back towards her home. I wanted to call to her, to ask her to stop, to give her a last goodbye-hug, but for some reason I didn't have the courage. We stood still for a while, watching her gray silhouette passing out of sight, and then, facing the direction in which we had to go, we trudged on in silence.

---

average annual official exchange rate, or 1250 kilograms of potatoes according to then-current prices.

Wife Beater

The fall was already coming to an end, gifting us with another cloudy day and a gray, smoky sky tightly lined with clouds. Trees had shed their leaves long ago, and now that fallen foliage was mixing up with dirt to make putrid, slippery slush. A little old waypoint station represented a colorless picture, reminding us somewhat of our foster home, and whispering into our ears that we would never escape its "house of desolation".

Not a single living soul was near that shabby, dingy box-office. We bought tickets to the nearest town and took the change, which I hid at once in the inside pocket of my quilted jacket while you kept the remaining money. We went out onto the platform. We had some time left before the arrival of a commuter train and, wrapping ourselves tighter in our blanket, we took a seat on the only bench there was. The time hung heavy; cold wind tickled our eyelashes and blew our hair. Soon there were four of us. A young couple appeared round the corner, came up and settled next to us.

"How long have you been waiting for a train?" the lady asked, slightly shrinking from the cold.

"Not so long," you answered.

"It should arrive soon," I added confidently, taking a look at the station clock. The train was due to arrive in less than half an hour.

"Do you smoke?" said the young lady. "Please, have a treat."

"Can we have two?" you took courage.

She looked at us for a while, then smiled tenderly and handed us over the whole pack.

A sudden freedom had liberated us. We weren't viewers any more but became fully legitimate life- participants. The lady behaved amiably, making jokes from time to time, and seemed to have forgotten her silent companion. I felt inexplicable bliss. Our usual awkwardness and constraint disappeared and was replaced by a feeling of general well-being; I was pleasantly dizzy from the tobacco smoke and let the great world spin by. Finally, the train approached. The young lady didn't even move but, on the contrary, took out another cigarette and lit it. We said goodbye politely and got into one of the steel wombs of this commuter train. After swallowing us up, it obediently moved out of the station, carrying away the fragments of hundreds of our old memories. Hundreds of eyes – tired, bored, lost or simply curious – gave us a stare in the carriage; they did it so harmoniously and coordinatedly that it was possible to think they belonged together and were acting as a unified organism skillfully pretending to be people. An elderly man sitting next to us thumbed through a newspaper, yawning and falling into a troubled sleep every now and then.

The commuter train was slowing down; the man was sleeping; I was reading the news in his paper out of the corner of my eye; you were staring out of the window. Everybody was busy with something or other, occupied or unoccupied at the same time. But once we approached our destination, people got anxious and started fussing and spilling out of the carriage, instantly dispersing, breaking off the threads that had connected all of us together. I watched them and thought that if you and I had not been so well tied together, who knows, maybe, we would have gone our separate ways as well. I snuggled closer to you, and we, full of determination, went into the station building where we were faced with yet another trouble. After standing in a long line and approaching the box office, all of a sudden, we found out that we had lost all our money! Not willing to draw unnecessary attention to ourselves, we quietly stepped aside and started searching. I rummaged through our food bag several times and you looked in your pockets. Nothing! Nothing but trouble. Our money had disappeared. There was nothing but the change we had received after buying the tickets, and, of course, our trampled-on hope.

Hope, tell me how it is possible that grief and happiness are scattered all over the world so unevenly? Why do some people get all the troubles and misfortunes while others are intoxicated with an abundance of material belongings, fat bellies and money? Why is there such injustice? Or are we mistaken that it's unfair?

The rest of day we spent wandering around the town, not having the strength to speak or to cry or even for that matter to feel sad. Deep in my soul I hoped for a miracle and thought that nobody could treat us so meanly and take from us our only real help; I humbly believed that somebody would surely come up and ask us: "Excuse me, did you drop this money?" But nobody did.

It was getting dark. Snow was falling in thick, heavy flakes and melting right under our feet, turning into slippery gruel. Patches of our dreams looking like these snowflakes waltzed in the light of lonely lanterns. We were wearily staring at the boring black-and-white scenery and, in a lousy mood, we strolled along the road into the gloomy emptiness, when a light in the distance from headlights struck our backs. We didn't look at where it came from, believing that no one in this world wanted to help us or care for us. But after driving past us a few extra meters, the truck stopped, the door opened, and a huge man with a moustache leaned out.

"Hey, where are you going?"

"To the capital," I uttered inertly.

"Home!" you grumbled to yourself.

"Me too," the man brightened up. "Get in; I'm bored of driving all by myself. I'll give you a lift."

Without thinking twice, we got into the truck.

"I'm dying to talk to somebody. What a goal I've scored to rustle you up like this," the man continued, getting excited about his own words. "I'm a lucky fellow."

The truck moved off. He called himself a "champion of the highway" and promised to deliver us to our destination "still canned goods". Despite an evening chill, he was wearing a wife-beater shirt of uncertain color, which probably had never been washed from the date of its purchase but had served him as a subject for boasting. Our entire conversation was essentially about it.

"What do you know! My whole life is daubed here," he said hoarsely and drawlingly and, pointing at some greasy spot, explained: "This one is from the borsch that Zinka, my mistress, cooked; a good bitch she was, but drunk herself to death. This one I got when Petrovich and I were pulling the truck out of a ditch, and he stuck his finger into the oil. And that one I had at my sis's wedding when I thumped my brother-in-law's mug. We made it up afterwards, though."

Despite the captivating story entirely devoted to such a sophisticated item of clothing as a wife-beater, we couldn't distract ourselves with any other subject. His dirty socks, noticeably stinking in the confined area of the cabin, didn't help matters, either, but being unaware of his fault, this champion of life continued to pour forth his wisdom, then suddenly he must have noticed our dismay, for he said:

"Yep, my feet really foul up the air so hard that you could cut it with a knife. I've tried alumen and talc but it doesn't help. Even my wifey couldn't get used to it. Everything in the house stunk; I couldn't breathe myself. That's why I became a trucker, all from hopelessness. My life could be quite different if not for this *little flaw*, my damned feet."

His entire story about his wife-beater and feet was accompanied by hoarse roars from his tape recorder resembling human voices, narrating tough life in a prison camp, while naked "wenches" on the windshield smiled at us, winking teasingly.

When the dead of night came, the champion drove into a special truck parking lot.

"Let's call it a day; we will spend the night here. I'm going to my fellow drivers and you park yourselves over there," and he waved his hand somewhere behind us, adding: "We're starting at eight tomorrow morning." And throwing on a leather jacket, he spilled outside.

The air in the cabin was stuffy. We lowered the window, took out our food, laid it out on the seats and started eating unwillingly, with no appetite. The only thing I was dreaming of was for this night to end soon and for morning to come. Behind the seats was a small berth; we got undressed and laid down on it, covering ourselves with the blanket. I always find it hard to fall asleep right away and at that moment in my mind I was scrolling through past memories – good or bad? It seemed to me that we had spent our entire short life up to now in special institutions, but for the first time we were facing the real world that we had only seen on the screen of a black-and-white TV (until it broke down). About that "real" world, I reflected, I hadn't a clue!

I was on the brink of falling asleep, when the cabin door briefly opened to let the champion in. To tell the truth, we didn't expect to see him so soon, let alone in such a state of intoxication. Scared, I squeezed myself into a corner and drew the blanket over my head. Meanwhile, he was swearing heavily and spitting on the floor, then he sat on the front seat and started fidgeting, shivering and breathing heavily. All of a sudden he got up and sharply pulled the blanket off us. I was struck by the combination of his wildness and our tameness, and I pressed myself into the berth, horrified not at what he might do to us but more at him seeing our deformity. I think you felt the same. But the champion didn't notice anything; he was panting and puffing right over me. I can still distinctly remember the terrible, alcohol-laden breath pouring from his mouth, and then this huge shapeless hulk lay on top of us with all his weight. We were powerless to cry out or to move; it seemed that my ribs were cracking under his pressure. At first I thought he might have forgotten that he had picked us up on the road and was simply following his usual routine, settling himself in his bed, getting ready to sleep, but when his fingers, like slippery worms, started crawling all over our bodies, I realized that he had it in for us. Everything happened very quickly. The next moment sharp pain pierced my body, and I felt someone else's flesh penetrating my flesh. Fighting with disgust, choking and swallowing my tears, I tried to escape for all I was worth, but with no luck. I don't know how long it lasted; my memory carefully hides from me everything that happened that night. I only remember that he suddenly stopped and started breathing rapidly and limply as if he were about to faint. At that moment I thought we were doomed, that we were going to die and be buried alive under his huge body. However, in a minute he regained consciousness, slowly slid on to the floor, took off his wife-beater in one movement, wiped off the after-effects of a rough night, and having lovingly put it under his head, fell asleep at once. New spots that had been left on his wife-beater became forever a part of its history which he would probably never remember to tell anyone about.

I had a throbbing sensation in my temples on both sides; it was hard to breathe; the air became stuffier and stuffier. I longed to strip off all my clothes and to pour cold water over myself to wash away the hurt, the pain and the humiliation. I remember the only question tormenting me was why I hadn't closed my eyes. Those memories are so repulsive; every time I think of them I feel just the same disgust as that night. I fell into a slumber and when I woke up, the ruthless world regained its outlines, muddy like stains on glass. I felt that you were also awake and expected you to give me a couple of words of support or consolation, but you did not speak, and I wanted you to die.

"Faith," after all, you curled your fingers around my wrist and whispered, "nothing happened. Do you hear me? It was just a disgusting nightmare. Remember, only a nightmare."

"A nightmare shared by both of us?"

"Yes, that was the only time we went through it together. This nightmare will never happen again. We will forget it once and for all. Do you understand me?"

"Yes," I nodded; and you have indeed forgotten everything, but not me.

In sleep, I heard an alarm clock ringing and opened my eyes. As if nothing had happened, the champion was sitting at the steering-wheel picking his teeth.

"Are you up already? Gee, how I managed to get drunk again yesterday."

We replied with unfriendly silence.

He scratched the clotted, sweaty thickets on his stomach with one hand while starting the truck with the other.

"So what's your name, gal?"

He addressed us both as if we were one person, thinking of us, beyond any shadow of doubt, as one whole creature.

"One..." you began spitefully but stopped short and turned away.

"I am Faith," I reluctantly forced out.

"Well, Faith, well, well," he grinned. "My mother's name was Faith, too; she passed away a while back. I used to hit her, but not from malice. Listen, kiddo, excuse me, if there was something wrong; I didn't mean it. It's all because of my feet, my damned feet."

The truck pulled away and the champion started a new story about his old wife-beater, as tiresome and boring as his entire life. And we kept silence as if we were angry at each other for the world being angry at us.

Back to the Ground

As we drove into the capital, we saw high brick buildings, wide, level streets, and huge monuments – overhanging, suppressing, frightening. A stray thought came into my mind: a person's life doesn't mean anything here. Everything seemed to be planned, designed and constructed to emphasize the insignificance of all your acts, thoughts and desires. It seemed useless to fight for anything because someone had decided it all for you ages ago.

The champion dropped us off near a subway entrance, and before leaving explained that it was a special place "to see new people and let them see you". Actually, the whole city was absolutely the same. However, at this point in time, we didn't have a clue what he meant, but being afraid to detain him in more conversation, for he would surely talk about his wife-beater status yet again, we didn't say a word.

Near the subway, an enormous exhibition complex was located. So, for the rest of the day we hung around it and measured it with timid steps. The uncaring wind pierced our lonely bodies; heavy gray and white clouds resembling patches of dirty cotton-wool were sternly etched into the sky above our heads, crawling into an unknown future. Thousands of people were flashing before our eyes in a roundabout of life, changing faces, moods and clothes, a whirlpool of giddy, useless action. It seemed that in a little while we, too, would get stuck in this huge, impenetrable mass and go round and round forever. That giant city swallowed us on our very first day there.

It started snowing. Having got out of the endless exhibition maze by a miracle, we wandered about the frosty streets, uselessly peeking in at yards, trudging gloomy back streets. And all the time, I couldn't get rid of an intrusive feeling that you knew where to go. At last, having come out onto a spacious street, we stopped near a crooked, abandoned lantern.

"It's late. We need to find a place to spend the night." You summed it up in a level, calm voice. "We will look for a hospital tomorrow."

I had seen an unlocked door to a basement. I decided to share all my observations with you.

"Where?" you revived, rubbing your hands together as an expression of joy.

"Round the corner in the backstreet; we passed it not long ago."

"Can you find the way?"

I nodded. We turned back and set out to search for that much desired lodging where we could spend our first night. I noticed a narrow tunnel that looked like it was leading to the underworld; behind it we could see a playground and the political leader's bust with a heap of snow on its spacious, bald head. Between two entrances, a hunched basement "crowned" with a withered door with a torn-off lock stuck out like an unnecessary knuckle. Nearby lay empty wooden boxes and broken bricks.

Like inexperienced thieves, we stealthily opened a door and glanced inside. Dampness and the stench of excrement invaded our senses; we saw low steps leading to… pitch darkness. "Feels like in a crypt," I said, thinking, "It's scary and unpleasant. I don't want to descend but I have to". That's how hardship and extreme conditions often force you into acting in a way that is completely alien to your usual way of behaving.

"You'd better stick with me," you whispered. Holding on to the walls, we moved down with extreme caution, literally by touch. Our eyes had adjusted by the time I found the switch and turned it sharply. A dim, unsmiling light illuminated a long corridor with a row of doors on each side, a concrete floor and a scattering of cats.

"Turn it off!" you hissed. "Someone may notice us."

I turned it off obediently, and the blinding darkness mantled us once again.

"Let's bring some boxes here and make a bed out of them," you commanded in a muffled voice.

I nodded and tried to do it to the best of my ability.

We spent the whole night in a half-dream. We turned around, lay down on our backs, and then rose to lie down on our stomachs. Wooden boxes squeaked plaintively and seemed to try to defend themselves from us, sticking iron parts into our bodies. Our night was miserable and dreary. Awakened by the morning light filtering through small windows under the ceiling, I lay on our improvised bed thinking how weirdly this life works, after all. We are sleeping on harsh boxes in a damp and musty basement, and meanwhile somewhere far away from here, people like us, conjoined people, may be living too; they have parents, study at a university, and fall in love, get married or even act in movies. They live a full life and we are fighting for our dishonorable existence, unwanted and rejected by everyone.

After getting up we had a substantial breakfast and immediately left the basement almost running, committed to never coming back. We wanted to forget this place as soon as possible. "It is a pity we didn't try to ask the champion where we could find a hospital to go to," I regretted while we were wandering about the well-trodden streets. Despite the cold weather, in many yards, elderly people were sitting on chipped benches or in sloping pavilions and were playing dominoes. With the accuracy of a measuring device, they poured port into glasses and drank it off, turning away as if in embarrassment. Their frozen faces got brighter and brighter pink, and their reputable game was gradually acquiring an ardent tone. We adjusted our blanket and approached an old woman hanging around a low, lopsided bench like a pigeon.

"Excuse me," you started as politely as possible while I secretly examined her wrinkled face, "could you please tell us where the nearest hospital is?"

"Why, what happened?" she responded, and others nearby looked at us with undisguised curiosity.

"No big deal, my sister's got a thorn in her hand," you lied determinedly.

"Oh, you should try to pick it out with a needle; let us take a look."

"Well, we've already tried to do it," I lied, hoping to save the situation, "but it's got stuck deep inside. I think we need to see a doctor."

"Oh, well, as you wish," the old woman drawled unsympathetically, seeming extremely annoyed at not having the chance to look at the "injury". "There is a polyclinic nearby. Go out of the yard, then turn left, walk about two hundred meters and you are right there. Do you need somebody to walk with you?"

"No, thank you a lot. There's no need to bother. We'll find a way," I apologized, guiltily staring at the tips of my felt boots. Awkwardly turning around, we went in search of this hospital, providing the old women with a hot topic for conversation.

Once we got out of the backstreet, on the first try we came across the white, three-storied building, a district polyclinic.

Everything seemed to be going as well as it could, and all our wishes and dreams soared up in our imaginations once again just like a while ago. We were going to succeed.

We entered the glass door and at that very same second we bumped into the tail of a very long line consisting mainly of elderly people reminiscent rather of delinquent schoolchildren than of patients. They were moving with enthusiasm and passion like young lovebirds doing a slow dance, then stiffening themselves against a small window – for some reason located at waist height – with an inscription which read "Reception Desk", and finally vanishing into the narrow gut of an ordinary corridor for good. A colorless female voice brought me back to my senses:

"Hey, I'm talking to you! Your first and last names?"

We named ourselves.

The receptionist turned around and started looking for a medical history sheet among numerous racks.

"I can't find any. Are you sure you have registered?"

"We don't have a medical record," I said uncertainly; "we're here for the first time."

"Then why are you playing with my head? Give me your passport," the same voice replied without any intonation.

We had to bend our knees and cave our backs in order to be able to see her, to hear the owner of such an emotionless voice.

"The passport... I've lost the passport," you lied.

"No passport – no record. As soon as you get the passport, you are welcome. Next." The last word was addressed to the queue standing behind us.

I couldn't believe what was happening. It seemed to be absolute high-handedness. Was there anybody to stand up for us? Would anybody help us? As time went by, nothing happened. People in the line shuffled forward, paying us no attention whatsoever. Dim, senseless, resigned. Is it so hard to offer your help and sympathy to somebody in grief? It takes a little to take one step, but, in an inexplicable manner, it stretches into thousands of kilometers. All of us are full of empathy and consolation but always prefer to express it from a distance.

"We will go to another hospital," you declared without hesitation, seizing me by the hand, forcefully bringing me to the bulletin board, pointing your finger at it.

"Do not panic. Here are the addresses of other hospitals; we will visit them all until we find one which will help us."

Despite all the difficulties we had encountered, the subway turned out to be the most invincible obstacle. I recollect it with irony. Ticket gates, like greedy gatekeepers, restlessly collecting fares, looked at us severely and formidably. We decided to take them by storm, but no such luck: metal hands clapped and closed on your hip. We didn't dare to ram the gates another time and just shuffled about beside them, disturbing the passers-by. At last the subway duty-officer, seeing our desperate attempts, kindly let us through an armless pass saying: "It's ok, but next time you should buy a ticket." We thanked her and stepped forward, but slowed down at once near the swung-open jaws of an immeasurable stone giant. People pressing from all directions instantly caught us up and dragged us down through the concrete arches of a gullet. Before we knew it, we were digested, satiating the stomach of the monster with a wild roar.

In the next hospital, no one would even listen to us. They requested our clinical record and waved us off once they heard that we didn't have any. People! Please. Listen. Our life, our bodies, are the most authentic clinical record ever! Why do you have to ask for any other, alien, fake, distorted by illegible handwriting, belonging to someone else who has never been us and has never tried to understand us? Do you think that is right?

I wanted to argue, shout, prove something, but I didn't get the chance. You firmly grasped me by the elbow and hastily said:

"Never mind, still, we're going to make it. Do you believe me?"

Of course I did. But, nevertheless, I had certain doubts about the possibility of such a surgery being performed, at least, not in the very first hospital we might address. We needed to find a genuine medical star, a brilliant scientist inclined to examine us and perform the separation. But memories of all the hardships we'd been through kept us from doing the right thing – going for the new, perhaps longer and more exhausting, course of action. We were eager to get separated at once, quickly and imperceptibly.

I nodded affirmatively. What else could I do? You have never asked me to share my thoughts with you, never wanted to know what I really felt deep down. You sped directly towards your goal, not mine. Telling you that the way you had chosen was wrong would be perceived as provocation. You were so passionate about it and really made us nearly fly to the other end of the city to find that hospital. Snow squeaked complainingly under the obstinacy of our feet.

"You can see the general practitioner without a preliminary appointment," another receptionist said dryly, filling in a form in fidgety handwriting. She didn't request our documents.

We left our overcoats in the cloakroom and, not parting with our blanket for a single second, went to the general practitioner's office. After waiting for a while in the line, we entered a quite close, intensely heated premise and saw a middle-aged woman in a white robe with a wrinkled nose and small eyes. On her desk there was a vase with one rose and plenty of papers and pens. She took her eyes off the perishing flower and started to study us hastily.

"Why are you coming in together? Come in one at a time."

Again this awkward situation! How might we explain briefly our predicament? Instead of arguing, we just took off our blanket.

Our deformity made the most painful impression on her. First she was surprised, then frightened; her small eyes became unexpectedly huge, expanding to fill half her face. For a long minute she plunged into painful reverie, then asked us to fill in a medical form, and went out of the office, but soon she returned in the company of a very short and scrawny man, the surgeon. Smiling and friendly, he at once suggested following him into his office. Well, considering all the circumstances, we took our folded blanket and followed him along the corridor.

Watching us closely, *in our natural condition*, some patients were immensely embarrassed while others stared without blinking, as if we were exotic animals, and spoke in a loud whisper that could be overheard.

"You are quite an extraordinary event in some ways," the surgeon said thoughtfully, attentively examining us in his office, "so rare as if we put two green beans into a bag with red beans, shook it well, poured out all the contents on to a table, and found the two green beans lying next to each other. What an interesting case."

Expressing this deep thought, he screwed up his eyes catlike, stretched, straightened and only afterwards looked at the form we had completed.

"Oh, my goodness, we share the same last name." He twitched his eyebrows several times and continued a bit less pompously. "It is a really extraordinary case. May I ask where *such special people as yourselves* are from?"

"It's a long story we've told too many times," you answered unwillingly.

"To cut a long story short, we came from a foster home," I said, blurting out the truth.

"You are extremely different, like me and my wife, but at the same time have much in common." He clicked his tongue, gave a whistle and continued to speak. "So, did you leave or escape? Actually, you don't have to answer that. Times have changed, but formerly I would have been obliged to inform the relevant authorities and you would have been sent back in the twinkle of an eye."

However, he didn't sound aggressive; his voice was calm and steady as if he was talking to an old friend.

"Now then, what do you count on?" he asked very dispassionately, moving some strange, cold smoothing iron along our stomachs.

"We want to be like everybody else, each of us by herself," you explained in a strange voice.

"Oh, really?" he smiled again. "And you decided it is easy to cut you in half just like a watermelon, didn't you?"

He went up to the window, stood there for a while, thoughtfully examining the roofs of the neighboring buildings, and seeming to address himself, said:

"Weather is just wonderful today. The sun's shining, soft snow lying everywhere; I like winter. But there are things that upset me: people keep coming in crowds to the hospital, medicine is scarce, personnel works in two shifts and gets angrier and angrier with the situation. A patient died yesterday and we didn't manage to save him. It's a really bad time for all of us. Besides, you have one liver, one for two. I am afraid we won't be able to perform such an operation in this hospital. I am a surgeon, not a wizard."

Then he distractedly approached the lonely chair, sat on it and lit a cigarette, repeating:

"You must understand. I am a surgeon, not a wizard."

The same thing, but in different words! Pyotr Ilyich had told us this in the foster home. However, not trusting anyone but ourselves, we had kept on poisoning ourselves with senseless illusions for many months like a revengeful wife who poisons her unfaithful husband with arsenic. We did not expect to face such reality, did we?

That's how we finally perceived our situation. Everything we did, the whole dangerous way we went through things, was in vain. Having run away from one place specially arranged for us and people similar to ourselves, we found ourselves in a place where we did not belong at all. We were undesirables, unplanned in this grass-roots system, and once it noticed us, it started rejecting us in every way. Only in our dreams could things happen the way we wished, but in reality the distance between what we wanted and what we got was so huge that it could never be overcome. We left that hospital a completely different person, two completely different people.

The House that... Built

All night long we roamed the lifeless streets and snow-covered yards; doors of basements were equipped with heavy locks, attics were nailed up and garages closed. Choking and gasping with frosty air, getting stuck and drowning in snow drifts, exhausted, frozen and ridiculous, we represented a genuine caricature of mankind. In order to save myself from going mad with desperation, I imagined us as the heroines of a book, assuring myself that whoever the author was, he wouldn't let us die before the final scene, and when all our hardships became insufferable, he would replace them with a happy ending. However, it did not really help. Passing the shining windows, I quietly envied other people's warm homes, safety and carelessness... and so the "advantages" of our union became more and more doubtful, illusive and fierce.

Our senseless wandering lasted till the frosty and cloudy dawn; snow resumed falling again. Wild and inhuman fatigue overwhelmed me, my strength ebbing away. I longed to sit down and fall asleep, but instead you continued quickening the pace desperately, as if running away from someone – perhaps from me? Of course, I'm a ballast, an animated anchor hardly shuffling my disobedient feet. Houses, streets and cars were rushing before us like a rapid, dizzy whirlwind; blood was flowing through my head, echoing in the nape of my neck with a dull pain; I felt terribly nauseous from our hurried walking. "I mustn't fall." The only thing I could do was to keep saying that to myself. "I mustn't fall, otherwise I'm dead – *we are dead.*"

Having given up counting time, I didn't know how many hours or days we had been recklessly rambling about the ice-cold city. Time got washed away and lost its meaning and sense. But we persistently kept moving forward, for there was no way back; I was convinced it would be better to die than start everything over again. Suddenly you pulled my head to yourself and almost cried in my ear:

"Faith, come round. We're there!"

"Where is there?" I was perplexed. How could we possibly get somewhere if we were going nowhere?

"Look that way. Can't you see?" We were the only ones out there, but you kept crying, making it more and more difficult to focus. "The house is empty; nobody lives there. Let's go inside. Hurry up."

The more I peered into broken windows and a wide open door, the more surprised I was, and I hardly trusted my own eyes. Where did a silent, lifeless house downtown come from? Was it by chance or was there someone continuously leading us on, purposefully, with a purpose known to him alone?

All of a sudden, a haughty wind spurted; the door squeaked plaintively and slapped before our noses. I got frightened and stopped, not wishing to enter the house, but then the door opened again and some unfathomable power nearly pushed us inside.

"I'm sleepy to death," you interrupted my thoughts. "Let's look for a place to perch ourselves. Tomorrow, we'll take a look around." And we marched up the stairs in search of lodgings for the night.

You never tell me what you see at night in your dreams; is there a place for me? Can this house and everything related to it turn out to be the fruit of a shared nightmare? I will surely ask you when you wake up.

We brought firm cardboard boxes from the lower floors, then tore and spread them on the floor, making a crude kind of bed. Despite the draft and the terrible cold, we drifted off into a peaceful and senseless sleep like newly imprisoned criminals who had nowhere left to run. However, in the middle of the night, all lower floors flooded with heart-rending barking; someone else was escaping from the cold in that huge house besides ourselves. There were dogs fighting over food in the stinging darkness, but it didn't disturb us. On the contrary, it was even calming. We were happy not to be alone.

When I woke up early in the morning, I pretended to be sleeping for some time, having a strong presentiment that something distressing, something unpleasant was going to happen, as though a big, heavy world was about to fall on our brittle shoulders as soon as we got up, but the more I restrained myself, the more I realized how hungry I was.

"I'm feeling pretty hollow," I said finally, figuring that hunger was a shared reality.

"We have some sausage from granny's supplies left," you reported in a vigorous voice. "It's time to get up!"

We stretched and rose lazily, trying to move without a sound, for we didn't want to draw the dogs' attention to us and our food. Yeah, we were really afraid that reckless pity would lead us to share our last bite with those who had nothing at all. Anyhow, we were lucky; those dogs did not smell our paltry supply, and we finished our sausage without being disturbed.

After getting on our feet and dusting ourselves down, we descended the staircase cautiously. Fortunately, there was nobody around. However, we discovered *something more valuable*: a wardrobe door with a broken mirror, a backless chair and a holey globe with seas and oceans faded from moisture; extra dampened cardboard boxes lay under our feet. We also found old, torn, broken belongings left behind till the end of time; each of them untouched by us, continued, with care, to store the memory of its owner.

We laid out the boxes to dry them, took the door with the mirror upstairs and put it near our so-called bedroom, leaning it against the wall. We diligently curtained the window with a dirty, ragged oilcloth so that the wind wouldn't rush into our "bedroom", and carried away some small rubbish to the first floor. From among other stuff we dug out a kettle powdered with snow, and put it on the chair we brought from downstairs. In the neighboring room we found a huge, wooden chest all covered with a thick layer of frosty dust; its lid was adorned with a fancy carving. There was no lock on it, but we didn't dare look inside; rather oddly, the chest evoked incomprehensible, primal fear. I suddenly thought that it kept something so frightening and powerful inside, real or imaginary, that we'd better not guess and not know anything about it.

"Let's not open it," I offered. "Who knows what's inside?" All things considered, we decided to leave the chest as it was – unopened.

But what was really important was that we committed a lot of time and effort to furnishing our dwellings, having avoided the temptation to focus solely on short-term goals. We carried up gramophone records, picture frames, old calendars and someone else's photos. By the evening we were so tired that we fell into the "bed" and were asleep in a couple of minutes. Only the next morning did we venture outside to look around. The house was surrounded by trees with bare branches; dim light from lanterns poorly lit the neighborhood. Tenacious hunger, like an insatiable leech, stubbornly sucked at our stomachs and disturbed our minds. We took several steps forward and then stopped indecisively.

"We'll have to ask food from people," I said quick-wittedly. "There will always be somebody who helps us because people are kind."

Back then, we didn't know that appalling changes affected not only our lives but the entire country's, which was literally falling apart, and no one had control over these changes.

We decided to beg right there in the street. However, everything went wrong from the very beginning. People avoided us like the plague, quickly passing by. For some reason, I didn't expect this to happen and wasn't ready for it; the trifles that passersby occasionally threw to us were not enough even to buy bread. Day by day, freezing through and through, oppressed by primal needs, humiliated by our piteous condition, we strolled miles around the city, running away from a pitiless hunger that stealthily walked in our footsteps. And all this time a distant, annoying voice drawlingly raged inside me through the pain. "How long can you bear this? Come on, Faith, sit in a snowdrift and die! It is easier to give up than to resist." And I would have surrendered *to the mercy of that winner*, if I had been alone.

After a month of suffering, we turned into two starved shadows with one common, almost animal need – to fill our stomachs. Depriving us of freedom, suppressing our minds, hunger etched particular thoughts in our heads, those concerning satiation. Our main, daily goal reduced to just sustaining ourselves. Like small mice, we sniffed the surroundings, listened to noises, shamelessly rummaged in the garbage; that is so gross to remember. People extremely seldom gave us charity; more often they poked or pushed us, displaying almost physical disgust in us, too. They must have had the same spiteful, repulsive feeling upon seeing us, and, moreover, I was imprisoned in a raging hatred whenever I happened to see happy people. I wanted to offend, punch or bite them all for the fact that they were feeling all right while we were perishing. How dare they laugh and be happy when we were in such misery? Each of them lived as if he or she was the only person on earth and nobody else existed; there were only houses, trees and faceless shadows around to fill the empty spaces everywhere. Or so it seemed to me in my deranged and alienated state.

Meanwhile, winter embraced the city, everything withered, and nature fell asleep. We were almost unable to see the sun in the sky; nights were frosty, shrouding the city with all-conquering ice. Merciless wind was destroying glimpses of life in everything around us. Days and nights rushed along, replacing one another; we were starving, freezing, humiliated. We hated everything and had no idea how to make our hatred meaningful. However, the nasty weather stayed with us all the way; one could think that such a fierce winter was created specially to wipe out Hope and Faith as freaks of nature.

Everybody knows that there is suffering, poverty and loss in the world, but those things seem to be somewhere far away from here, until destiny or our own thoughtlessness make them evident. And once they are faced, we get scared, shout and resist, but all in vain: nobody notices us or everyone pretends we don't exist. When this happens, the main challenge is not to go mad with horror and despair.

"What shall we do, Hope? What can we do?" I lamented. "Maybe we should stop hiding in our blanket and show people what we actually look like? Let's try to visit private apartments and ask dwellers for help." You made no answer, as if you didn't hear the question, but the following day you offered the same advice. This being settled, we got rid of the blanket.

Shocked dwellers slammed their doors in our faces, or more often they didn't open them at all; thus their callousness was complete. So, is there any sense in *exposing yourself* to people if all you get is humiliation and pain? I want to know! Is it human nature to take offence or become annoyed or irritated when someone asks for help? Nobody likes being troubled by other people's problems. Yes, we had nothing else to do but to eat the food left for homeless animals in stairways and alleys.

I remember us hunkering down a staircase and eating the food scraps a dog had refused to eat. Suddenly the door behind our backs opens, and a man throws out a loaf of stale bread... It fell rumbling down the stairs. Like wild animals, we dashed to pick it up, not caring if someone was watching us and laughing when we looked back; we were already used to such an attitude even if I still believed people should treat us like humans. In the infinite succession of indignities and injustices that befell us and our half-starved existence, it seemed to be an absolute, incontestable norm that what had happened in the foster home should logically spread to our wretched lives outside of it.

A loaf of stale bread is a very valuable meal – odd that we had never thought about it earlier; if you consume it inexpensively it can suffice for a couple of days. First we broke the bread into several parts, cautiously hid them in our pockets, and then began to eat. I held each piece in my mouth for some time, soaking it with saliva, and had a strange feeling that the man was standing behind the door and still watching us through a peephole, waiting for something else to occur. But I couldn't care less, it wasn't important anymore; absolutely everything was unimportant.

Look, Hope, what if people refused to give us alms not because of disgust or irritation; what if they were ashamed to denigrate us by giving us the leftovers intended for animals? I can't help thinking of people better than they actually are. There may be no other way to share the good, really.

The next day we became witnesses of another incident. An elderly man, who was just passing by, stepped on a footless beggar sitting near the store, totally by accident. Maybe someone pushed the gaffer from behind or he simply didn't notice the man sitting under everybody's feet, I can't tell precisely; however, he nearly fell and, in anger, started caning his limbless "offender". How interesting the situation was: one person stepped on another and, instead of apologizing, beat him and everyone just stood around and did nothing. I remember that the only thing occupying my mind then was the can of alms that had rolled, scattering coins on the trampled snow. It took great restraint to stop ourselves from rushing to collect that beggar's earnings but that moment marked our fall, so desperate had we become that we were ready to steal even from a poor, beaten-up, disabled guy.

We spent two, long, winter months between life and death. At night we stayed in the abandoned house whose walls had already become home for us, for our flesh and for our blood. During severe frosts we would make a fire in a tin basin, burning pieces of old furniture scattered around. Our blanket kept getting covered with snow and hoarfrost, so we constantly had to dry it. We also hung up a kettle over the fire and boiled thawed icicles in it; we often drank hot water to prevent ourselves from catching cold. Looking at the burning wood, I tiredly closed my eyes and imagined a real home, cozy and warm. Before going to bed, we had to tie woolen shawls tightly round our heads and wrap up in the blanket. At daybreak, the fire died away, after which our "bedroom" became prisoner to frost and gloom; our broken mirror grew white with hoarfrost; tattered, dampened plaster hung down from the ceiling, the wind blew into cracks, water in the kettle froze up; and white death led by the blizzard walked stately about the house.

February was coming!

One early morning you forcibly woke me up and complained of a sharp belly-ache. I wasn't surprised at all, for our diet was scarce and loathsome; at times we ate scraps that had definitely gone bad. I got worried that you might suffer the same fate as Half-Jane. I decided to get up, but you only turned your head away and continued lying in dour silence, ignoring my requests, so all I could do was lie down and rest till noon. At last, your pain diminished, replaced by gnawing hunger, renewed vigorous stomach-cramp. Weak and clumsy, we managed to put on our quilted jackets and to go down the stairs but froze on the spot! Between the second and the third floors, we saw a girl, very young, with her head unnaturally thrown back and her eyes open. She didn't move, keeping enigmatic silence, feeble tenderness clinging to her lips. She looked as if in a moment she might make a movement, get up or say something... but that impression was deceptive. The girl was dead.

"I can't stand this anymore." Your voice ripped through the silence like a jagged knife. "It is better to die like she did than to live like animals do."

"What are you talking about?" I countered fearfully, shivering all over with icy presentiment. "What are you going to do?"

"Haven't you understood yet? The surgical operation won't change anything. We have been nothing more than animals and we will stay that way. We will spend all our life attempting to get food, even after our separation. We had a bad start."

Your words were frightening and repelling, but somewhere deep down in my heart I felt that you were right. However, a part of me was still in disbelief and voluntarily leaving this life was unacceptable. How could we reach a point where everything had no sense at all and there was no purpose left?

"Just look at her. She is happy!" and, clasping my face in your hands, you forced me to look that way. "She's already got nothing to worry about; she doesn't suffer from cold anymore and doesn't care where she can get a grub. *Now* she doesn't give a damn about anything."

"She is free," I repeated to myself, staring at her stiffened face. Is a primitive escape from life the only way to gain our freedom? Isn't there some other way?

"We'll jump out of the window." You said it so confidently as if you had reflected upon the thought hundreds of times before. "The house is high enough and we will definitely fall to our death. Just think about it, *this time* we will make the decision completely by ourselves. *For the first time* we will be personally responsible for our fate; it's the only thing we have got left."

Indeed, people are equal only in one thing. Every one of us is gifted a life; other differences are only notional. What to do with our lives is at our own discretion. The time had come to bestow upon us the most exalted gift of serenity and joy. We silently trudged back upstairs. I fancied that I heard steps creaking and groaning throughout the entire stairway as if hundreds of invisible feet were stepping on them along with us. We were still alive, but among the ghosts already.

It was snowing outside; the iron ledge boomingly tapped in the blasts of wind huffily breaking into the house that had sheltered us from death. At the window I hesitated for a moment, desperately vacillating between imminence and fear.

In my mind, multiple questions were replaced by new ones. What is the point of living if we are going to die anyway? What difference does it make if it's going to happen now or later? All we have to do is to take a step and jump off; that will resolve all problems, answer all questions once and forever. And what if we are *already flying down*? We have jumped off – perhaps, right after birth – not even knowing about it! The ground is already near; we just have this last moment *to live* and then we are finally released and we realize we are already *dead*, and had been from the moment of birth.

It is hard to take this last step, but the hardest thing is to face the choice between the unwillingness to live and the inability to die. With mixed feelings of horror and unshakeable determination, we stepped on the chest, and then got up on a window-sill. The wind was blowing mercilessly, trying to stop us, restrain us and push us back. I looked down, hoping for a quick death but not wishing to die. To jump off, stupid intention is not enough; one also needs to have courage. Who, then, is a suicidal person, a courageous guy or a fool? I might decide this for myself while flying down to earth, I reflected sourly.

I got dizzy. My hands were shivering frantically, my heart beat, my thoughts were confused and flashing; I was terrified by the thought that the end was near, so unexpectedly near. The wind picked me up and started shaking me aggressively. I realized all the futility of our existence, but down there, everything seemed much more senseless. I wonder what you were thinking at that same moment; you never told me. Not knowing what to do, I closed my eyes and imagined us lying on the ground, painting the snow with our blood, powerless in view of what we had done. Chilling frustration burdened me like a stone; my feet stiffened. In deepest confusion, I seized the window-frame with my hands and, yelling like I have never done before, pushed off the window-sill with my feet.

I remember that I fell on my back and screamed either with back pain or with relief. And at the same moment, I heard a groan of disappointment and rage: you were still alive, still here with me. Exhausted and satisfied – while standing on the window I held my breath with fear – I couldn't recover it for a long time, convulsively gasping for chilling air. Fortunately, our falling downwards had failed. Yeah, humans behave so strangely and miraculously, preferring life full of anguish to a quick end, clinging like grim death to something that brings pain. Each imprisoned by her own thoughts, we lay on the floor without movement like turtles turned upside down. At last, weakened by our unexpected rescue, you started crying bitterly, while I senselessly looked around to observe our refuge anew. There were times when life and love reigned in this house, but now it was undoubtedly dead; my eyes slid over intensely chipped beige walls, a long spiral staircase with a wooden handrail, huge semicircular windows and a fireplace still intact by some miracle. Apparently, many years ago the house served as a happy safe haven for several families, careful and grateful. Now, dilapidated, cold, abandoned, it breathed life into us. Sometimes, in order to start all over again one needs to step back, not forward.

And then the very next moment I caught sight of a chest lying near our feet. The longer I looked at it, the more perplexed I became. How could it be that we hadn't taken a look into it before? We didn't know what was in there. I had to do something right away and put thousands of thoughts into one promise. Fighting the pain in my lower back, I stretched out for the chest, gently lifting the lid and nearly cried out. There were books inside, plenty of books. A feeling of incredible freedom overwhelmed me, and having opened the very first one in the middle, I pretended to be reading, sliding my glance along each line and making out my own story in the process:

"A very long time ago, when the earth was inhabited by centaurs and unicorns, there also lived beautiful, two-headed people. As the millennia passed by, they built houses and cities and lived happily ever after. But there came a time when the two most beautiful women who were joined together gave birth to an unusual girl. As soon as she came into the world, she had two mothers but they grew numb with disgust. Their daughter had *only one head.* "How ugly she is; the gods must have cursed us," one of them uttered and burst into tears. All night long the women were inconsolable but at daybreak, after arguing for a very long time, they finally decided to take the terrible child into the woods and leave her there though they were well aware she wouldn't be able to survive alone...."

I paused to take a deep breath and turned the page over listlessly. You had already stopped crying and looked at me in astonishment, believing each and every word; and I believed together with you. Of course I did, for all this wonderful story was about us and was meant to be universal!

"And what happened to her?" you whispered quietly, still sobbing.

"She managed to survive. Trees gave her shelter from heat and cold, wild animals brought her food, she satiated her thirst with water from a river. Some time passed; the girl grew up strong and healthy and gave life to a whole race of one-headed people who populated all the earth and still dwell here."

"And where do you think the two-headed people have gone?"

"Gods really cursed them. They gifted two-headed people with a miracle, but none of them was able to appreciate it and got rid of it as if it was something useless and shameful. Eventually, the two-headed race completely disappeared. Yet gods, sometimes reminded of it, send another miracle to the earth."

I slammed the book closed and before putting it back into the chest, glanced at its name, which read "The Gulag Archipelago".

"We are a miracle, but miracles secretly inspire people with fear," you whispered reverently and, keeping silent for a little, asked: "So were there times when *all* people looked like us?"

"Yes. Probably that's why loneliness is so hard to bear."

"And as for us, we don't even happen to know what it is," you smiled with significance.

Who knows, perhaps the sense of our life lies in reconciling and getting used to the fact that we are different from everybody else; everyone is different.

"We don't need to be free from torments; we need to be free for the sake of the one-headed people," I said and started rummaging among those books in the hope of finding another miracle. The chest was filled with books, only books, down to the bottom, but you seemed extremely delighted by this.

"Finally, we have paper for our daily needs. But first you should actually read them," you added after thinking a while, and suddenly remembered the other poor girl, her murdered body. "And now, since we are alive, we must take care of the one who is dead."

Throwing the blanket over our shoulders, we went downstairs. The girl lay in the same place, lonely and untouched. Large flakes of snow were flying inside, through the broken window, falling, covering her cold body. They didn't melt. I dipped into contemplation once again, scrutinizing her silent face. Her long, messy hair was matted and stuck to her neck;

the salt of her last tears was visible on the skin-surface around her eyes. A wild, inhuman curiosity overcame me; I was eager to know why she had cried at the end of her life! Your voice pulled me out of my reflections.

"Let's carry the body to the neighboring house and leave it there in the basement or inside the stairwell."

"That would be improper," I said calmly. "That would be wrong."

"And what do you suggest? She won't walk away on her own two feet ever again."

"We could have been in her place just a short while ago," I continued, " walking on that "hell-bent" path, and I definitely wouldn't like us to be treated that way."

"I think we wouldn't care in that case. It is a dead body! Someone got rid of it and dumped it on us, so now we have the right to act the same way."

"That would be improper." I just repeated my own words. "Hope, listen. I've always given you the privilege of making decisions for the two of us. Now, let me do what I deem correct."

You sighed and sniffed.

"Do you suggest burying her?"

I shook my head.

"It's impracticable. The ground is hard like stone; we can't dig into it, and besides, we haven't got a shovel."

"So what shall we do?" you cried impatiently.

"We'll look for a militiaman and tell him we entered the house by mistake and came across a dead woman inside."

"So, another lie?" you quipped. "Well, quite okay with me!"

I wanted to object, but then suddenly understood: no matter if we looked at the world with your eyes or mine, it didn't change the essence. We lied constantly because we were forced to lie; our small lies were only a reaction to the big lies. All I could do was comfort myself with the thought that it will be another minor lie, intended to hide the unwanted truth.

The story we had made up in haste and apprehension, of course, didn't help us. At first everything went "according to plan". We found a militiaman and showed him where the girl's body lay. A huge guy with a baby face and a big belly dexterously rolled up the poor girl's sleeve and revealed injection spots on her arms in no time at all. It emerged that similar incidents had occurred quite often in our house. He called a patrol car via portable radio and took us to the dispatch center. Failing to provide a clear story and documents, we immediately got thrown into a slammer[14]. Everything happened so quickly that before we had time to realize it, we found ourselves behind bars and every employee of the dispatch-center any old time approached us without any pretext and stared at us like zoo visitors.

"We are so fucked up!" you hissed spitefully and defiantly turning away from me, moving your head only.

"You probably swallowed your gold crown today, for you're making such a fuss about yourselves," someone hoarsely laughed in the corner. "I see money, lots of money you're going to make," continued the same voice, "but it still won't help you; it gives you so many problems and so much grief and no love."

"It would be even more disheartening to know that we don't give a damn about love," you snapped. "And what were you saying about money?"

"You win some, you lose some, never know what you're gonna get," the voice chuckled.

---

14   Slang - pre-trial detention center; special premise for detainees in a police station.

It was very dark in the corner of the cell and so we couldn't make out the person talking to us. However, when our eyes got used to it, we saw a very stout, elderly woman, wrapped in a multitude of shawls. She was sitting opposite us and smoking a pipe.

"Are you a gipsy?" I asked shyly, examining this unusual woman.

"Me? Is that important? It is more important who you are. Answer this question, and everything will become clear."

"We are miserable freaks," you blurted out vehemently.

"We are all freaks. We are born normal, but gradually, step by step, things change," and she burst out laughing loudly. "It is a pity that you make no use of your own beautiful look; people would appreciate it and would not spare money."

"That's damn lies", you objected resentfully, "First, people are afraid of us, then they despise us, then they ridicule us, and then they ignore us."

There came a short silence during which the gipsy beat out ashes from her pipe and, having filled it again, came up to us closely.

"In fact being *so beautiful* isn't all good," she grinned mischievously. "My precious, I see fear and hostility in your words. You don't need to be afraid of people, they are afraid of themselves quite enough. What do you see around you?"

"A cell with grids; we are locked in."

"And unhappy," I added.

"And you probably think that after getting out of here, you'll suddenly become happy."

"We will be free," you replied defiantly.

"Will you?" the gipsy grinned. "Yes, your burden is heavy: unhappy, ugly, naive and miserable. However, the one who calls you so is miserable too."

I remember I thought then: "It seems like we are lucky again, meeting a person treating us like people".

"Do you think happiness depends upon other people or, maybe, upon so-called freedom?"

"Happiness... unhappiness," you snarled. "Who cares? We are locked up like animals in a cage."

"Yes, you are. You are right about it, precious. But this place is warm and they give you food and a bed. Maybe everything isn't so bad. That's a lot to think about," the gipsy said, puffing a stream of spicy smoke into our faces.

Having cleared my throat from the smoke, I tried to look at her closely and suddenly realized that she was absolutely blind. Her two muddy fish- eyes looked directly at us, and I could swear she could see with them.

"This place can't be good, that's why we feel bad," you noted acidly.

"Good... bad... It's neither bad nor good," imitating you, she muttered. "It depends on what it's good or bad for and how you get used to it. As for me, it's not only daylight that I can't see, but my old ass, too."

"In that case, everything that is good can turn out to be bad one day," I said for no obvious reason.

"It can... It cannot," the gipsy smirked. "Surreally, *it can't!*"

And having closed her blind eyes, she trudged back to her place in the depths of the cell.

Lower World

We spent all night long in the cell feeling cold and restless. I automatically rummaged around, always looking for something. In the dispatch center that never sleeps, I was forgetting and remembering again and again: they didn't give us our blanket back.

In the morning, an absolutely unfamiliar man, who looked as if he had a huge pug[15] instead of his head, with thick whiskers resembling furry paws and short ears covered with wool-like hair, came for us.

"Those ones!" he barked through clenched teeth to the militiaman accompanying him, pursing his lips as if he were getting ready to spit. "There is no need to make something up, they're model freaks; the money will just roll in."

And having blown his nose on the floor, the "pug" continued addressing us directly:

"Congrats! You've got a job: standing in a walking tunnel. Hey, don't make that face; to tell the truth, there's not much choice: either going with me or staying here in jail. And don't forget to thank Shanita for helping you."

We needed to make a decision. In search of advice, I looked around but saw no one. The bench in the depth of our cell was empty; the gipsy, probably the same Shanita, had miraculously

---

15   Decorative dog breed traditionally held by the aristocracy. A dog with a lively, cheerful, yet even temper, noble and affectionate to the owner.

disappeared. The only sound to be heard was the snotty pug's voice:

"The treatment of detainees at militia stations might actually be worse than in prisons."

We hesitated, but we really had no choice.

"Deal," you agreed.

In half an hour we were brought to a tunnel where some cripple was already standing with his knees slightly bent and his head tilted sideways. Thrusting his only hand forward, he squinted intensely, as if from blinding sunlight, and smiled mildly. As we came nearer he put his hand to his face convulsively, as if protecting himself from invisible blows, and started shivering miserably. Meanwhile, the pug whispered something in his ear, making the one-armed beggar screw up his face, which became small and sloped. A minute later he picked up his can from the floor, poured its contents into the pug's pocket and obediently left the tunnel, casting fearful glances around.

"Now this is your spot," the supervisor told us. We didn't know yet that that was what people collecting tribute from beggars were called – supervisors! Dwellers of and in the tunnels – cripples and the poor – literally worshipped the pug. He endowed them with a spot, and having a spot ensured, they didn't die, and food and a roof over their heads were guaranteed.

"There's no spot for us," you murmured in disbelief.

"Don't play stupid," he barked and handed us a can that had emerged from his hands and seemingly out of nowhere.

"Nobody will give alms to us; besides, we don't know how to beg," I said.

But instead of answering, the supervisor burst into loud laughter, which made the giant pug substituting for his face shake jerkily on his shoulders.

"If everybody knew how to beg, half of this country would stand in the tunnel. Don't look them in the face until they give alms; and when they throw a coin, raise your head, and shed a tear; they love it. I will come for money in the evening."

He took our blanket away so everyone could see. Some people feel ashamed – those immediately turn away and reflect on the injustice of the world; others, on the contrary, look at us with aversion, spit near our feet with defiance and go their way, but there are also those who feel pity easily and quantify it in monetary terms. That's our target public.

And, indeed, there were a lot of sympathetic people, and coins rained into our can. Well, it couldn't have been any other way. After all, they are *normal*, and we are not; and they had to pay for the difference!

After getting used to it a little, we found three other cripples standing along the wall at a distance. They were really unlucky: true cripples who, by a twist of fate, managed to turn their grief into a profession playing a social role on people's consciences. But however long I watched them, I couldn't find that intangible borderline where their lameness ended and their real acting began. Over time, their faces were no different from the unsightly masks they wore.

Many of them could easily have run away, but they didn't; on the contrary, they stood in the dirty tunnel every day as if in the line of duty, begging from people they despised and enriching others they hated. From the very beginning, their fate was obvious: to perish and thereby create space for others to take their place, those more lame. And still they didn't hurry to die, demonstrating incredible miracles of longevity, clinging to life by all means possible; and the more worthless it was, the more unwilling they were to leave it.

At first I was constantly pursued by a quiet, pitiful pleading of my inner voice that kept telling me: "Quit it, Faith. Get up off your knees. This is not what you came to this city for. Where is that inquisitive girl spending her days with piles of books? Where is the girl dreaming of beautiful feelings day and night? Have you lost the last bit of your dignity?" Yes, I lost everything. I have nothing left but this animal instinct to survive. I lost my pride; my soul is trampled and crippled. This is the bottom. I am not a human being any more. The people passing by are merely obliged to point their fingers at us and to scoff at us, not hiding their disgust. With my head hung down and my arm stretched out, I was almost looking forward to new humiliation and pain, but soon, to my great surprise, I found out that this entire crowd actually didn't care about us at all. That brought me relief and a certain freedom. Earlier, I happened to watch a small river flowing in the wood where we were roaming in search of a shelter from rain and people, or a natural turnover of inmates in the foster home; now, I see a gloomy, impenetrable flow of half-poor people rich in fake compassion; everybody is in a senseless hurry, drearily moving in space.

* * *

Several months passed; we got used to standing in the tunnel and felt at home. And everything would have been good but for a rampant and unrestrained boredom. Having nothing better to do, we counted and recounted our "old acquaintances" – white spots of faces floating by, whom we met on a daily basis. We recognized some of them by their walk, others by the clothes they wore, and others appeared so regularly that they could serve to synchronize watches. Every face was different, but they all were unified by a strange similarity, that is, by an indifference to the world around them. And if somebody put two dolls in our place, threw two quilted jackets over them and made them stretch their hands forward, nobody would notice the difference. That's how it goes. It's easier to close your eyes than to ruin your life with risky and unattractive truth. We catch indifference like the flu from each other: symptoms are different, but the consequences are always the same and catastrophic.

Most often, however, we met passersby for the first time; they gave us a glance not expressing any sort of surprise; their eyes were disinterested and bored; not a single urge enlightened their "blind" faces. It is hard to believe, but owing to such "day-flies" I quickly got used to being in the public eye and started seeking people's company from an urge of my own. Thus, having become conspicuous, from an ugly burlesque of humans, we turned into ordinary twins. There's a certain magic in it, don't you agree? It turns out that conjoined people aren't so unnatural. They are just a strange whim, a kink in nature, deviation that doesn't seem to exist but is encountered every day.

All day long we were acting out ecumenical grief and humility, but I didn't really feel anything of that kind, though I tried my best. In order to correspond to the "beggar's iconic image", I always raised my head submissively when people were throwing us money, and thanked them. Donors truly believed that by giving alms they were doing something very significant and well-timed, which fed their egos. Like a wooden idol in a temple, we had nothing but to play mute, accepting other people's donations and "absolving sins". However, I don't claim to be an angel speaking the undeniable truth; these are just the ordinary thoughts of unordinary people among ordinary people.

When we got bored with counting familiar and unfamiliar faces, we went further and created various roles for ourselves: you pretended to be a stutterer and I shook my head like a madman. Once we had immersed ourselves completely in these roles, we roared with laughter; I guess we were heard throughout the tunnel. It's an odd thing, but that attracted far more people to us than usual, and the amount of coin in the beggar's can doubled.

So, gradually, the real world existing outside the tunnel and the world in which we lived became less and less disturbing, reaching us only by "people flashing" and by small memory ripples. We were very well aware that just several hundred yards away, literally on the neighboring railway platform, real life was in full swing every moment of every day, and that somebody met someone else or saw someone off; couples embraced each other, kissed and swore eternal love but at the same time, they were as far away from us as though they inhabited a different solar system. Meanwhile, our lower world was full of eternal melancholy: stubborn people glimpsed like shadows, hurrying about their important but useless errands, exchanging their lives for trifles and mistakes.

Nevertheless, the two worlds sometimes came closer to each other. I remember we once stood on our usual spot when a family passed by: two twin girls of about fourteen with their parents. They weren't even going but floating in such a manner that one could be forgiven for believing they had come for a walk in the tunnel. Taking their time and totally captivated by each other, they didn't seem to notice their surroundings and their brutal reality. Their parents were holding hands, whispering gently to each other like a couple of lovers; their faces radiated happiness, lighting up everything around. First the twins didn't notice us but then we met. What a surprise it was to see pure, sincere compassion in their eyes. It seemed like our looks pulled the girls out of their habitual lives and showed them that reality, after all, *can be this way*. It lasted just a moment, whatever it was: one saw grief, and the other hope. It is impossible to believe that one single event can give rise to such different emotions.

* * *

Our working schedule was similar to that of the rest of the country, five days a week; from early morning we stood in the tunnel, incessantly making ourselves and any impressionable passersby uncomfortable. On our days off, looking for something to occupy myself with, I started reading the books we had found in the old chest. The process turned out to be so exciting that soon I couldn't stop. I was reading constantly – while you were sleeping, in the subway or in a store, at home in the light of a street lamp – anywhere I could seize a spare moment and a clear space. I had the unshakeable feeling that these books had been specially written for me and put into the chest so that I could find and read them.

Little by little, out of my own "pocket library", I learned that our world is full of stories about love and hatred, about beautiful things and ugly things, about good and evil. Each has his predetermined fate allotted him. Those few who get lucky and are born good-looking are conferred the part of hero, and those who are less lucky or completely unlucky are given very unattractive parts: despicable villains, outcasts, or worse. And it doesn't matter what I am inside my soul; what leads me to preserving the human essence is not in my head, not even in my heart – but it doesn't matter! Doesn't matter at all...

And while I devoured books, you looked around suspiciously, obviously bored. I tried in every possible way to involve you in the reading process, but nothing worked. Despite the fact that we are twins, moreover conjoined twins, and must have a lot in common, we often didn't talk for long hours. Being not alone physically, none the less, I felt lonely from time to time. And that was how a whole year passed; it seemed as though time had frozen up. However, there wasn't even the slightest sign of integration. I was changing, you were changing, and everything around us was changing.

The supervisor who took us out of prison turned out to be a disgusting type, but due to necessity rather than pleasure. The pug where his head should have been looked at everybody with glistening and, at times, tear-stained eyes, always clouded with indifference and boredom. With gloomy constancy he tried to inspire us with respect and fear, but instead he evoked only hatred and open hostility. Actually, there was nothing mindless or cowardly about him, neither great nor terrible, but the total absence of everything. Twice a day he collected a tribute from all the beggars who, uncomplaining and unanimous, emptied pockets before him. However, we kept a part of our earnings – our "due" wages.

Very soon we started making a substantial income for the pug. Because of that, our "colleagues" (other cripples in the tunnel) were continuously furious and jealous, for now people were throwing us *their* money – the money they could have made and must have wanted. Possibly, in revenge for success or probably just "pro forma", we were nicknamed Hydra. Naive blunderers. Didn't they understand that we had got used to such treatment from childhood? The only person who really liked us was the hero of the Patriotic War, a disabled old man from the house across the way. He came into the tunnel three times a week, on odd days, never even. On the other days, he could be seen at a cemetery where he brought flowers to the graves of his family. In the tunnel he was begging like everybody else.

However, he was an independent person, not subject to supervision. People still kept up the appearance of conscience, so no one dared to call him a bad name. Having paid his military due to the homeland, he proved to his full extent that he was worth any place, even the money-making tunnel. However, passersby seldom gave him alms, for he had an inappropriate, proud look. He'd lost his legs in the war, one of them completely, and the stump of the other ended somewhere at knee-height. While other legless beggars sat on low, wooden platforms with four wheels at their corners, he moved around in an old wheelchair, dexterously manipulating it with his strong hands. Everybody called him Ivan. Just Ivan. He didn't wish to hear either his patronymic, or his last name. He looked about seventy years old, always clean-shaved, neat and tidy. Cleanliness was essential to him, and we got along with him well.

"If you want to survive, you should not get sick; and in order not to get sick, you have to keep your body clean," he used to say.

He lost all his family long ago: his brother and his father were shot by the chief authorities, his mother died of typhus. His reason for living existed far back in the past, and a lonely death awaited him in the present. However, he actually wanted to die and lived in anticipation of death, not distracted by life's hardships and not frittering away his strength with futile feelings.

Having noticed that we were constantly scratching ourselves, he immediately suggested we take a shower at his house. Tormented by remorse, we nevertheless agreed very quickly because this trivial option to be clean, readily available to almost everyone, was a great blessing to us. Surprisingly little is known about how often happiness can depend on such absolute trifles.

Ivan lived in a communal apartment[16]. Not wishing to disturb his neighbors, he used to bring us to his place only at night. Every time he gave us two towels. Honestly, I'd got out of the habit of being treated like that and instinctively waited for some kind of wild game trap, but he turned on the tap and waited next to the shower-room door, watchfully guarding the entrance.

"At least I have a place to live, thanks to the government," he comforted himself thinking out loud. "They promised to grant us separate apartments, but I've been waiting for that for about twenty years. It's all right; I don't want to complain... it is what makes us human."

Strong affection often grows from dependence, and after all, you and I really depended on him; there's no reason to deny it. Nevertheless, there was something bigger between us than the usual attachment and gratitude; it was true friendship, though unfortunately very short. I remembered him as an incredibly responsible person, living in strict accordance with his schedule; therefore, when he didn't appear in the tunnel, we knew the reason right away: the old man's wait was over. He lived like few people do but died like everybody else.

Meanwhile, the country sank deeper and deeper into an atmosphere painfully reminiscent of our tunnel, where nobody

---

16   Communal apartment - an apartment where several families dwell in isolated premises. Each family or individual person occupies one or several rooms, sharing "common areas" which generally are a bathroom, toilet and kitchen as well as a corridor and a hall.

believed in anything and nobody trusted anyone. People traded all they could: veterans sold their awards, actresses adored by millions of fans across the country offered their hungry bodies and even those who did not have anything bartered what remained of their conscience for money.

In our crippled country, we ceased to be cripples.

Alive

That year's "abundant" events agitated the whole country. But also something minor, personal and very amusing happened at an odd moment. We still had to sleep in the abandoned house, which we diligently returned to every evening. One fine evening, tired and exhausted after standing on our feet all day, drenched to the skin and dreaming only of lying down as soon as possible, we got home... and suddenly our routine was interrupted, crushed. As we entered the house, we found uninvited guests sitting near a fire that they had kindled. They were arguing about something, trying to outshout the thunder peals; it was lashing down outside, lightning lit the sky. Nature stormed in its heart. Despite fatigue, we were in an excellent mood; I always loved a thunderstorm, for it washed all my troubles away.

First they didn't notice us and continued to argue awkwardly. We strained our ears to listen.

"Let's start!" one of them commanded. "It fell on heads."

"Why is it heads? Maybe we should... well, flip the coin one more time?"

"We've already flipped! I'm starting: first I will stab you, right in the heart, and then myself. Are you backing out?"

"No... I just thought we'd... well, let's flip it one more time," and, shivering with fear or with indignation, he picked up the coin from the ground, but never flipped it.

Because we, Faith and Hope, like two ghosts, appeared before them in the doorway like two of nature's spontaneous apparitions. I had got used to all the weird things mentioned in books and wasn't surprised at all by absolutely incredible matters, yet those boys shocked us unimaginably at that moment. At first they stared at us with eyes made huge by astonishment, and then in a couple of moments they dashed in opposite directions. One of them stumbled and almost fell into the fire and the other unsuccessfully tried to get out through the window. We never laughed so loudly in all our lives, not anywhere – not even in the tunnel. Our laughter could be heard from afar, too, and helped those unfortunate refugees near us to understand that we were alive. And apparently, we had involuntarily disrupted their plans.

"How did you get here?" you asked, weeping from laughter.

"We're just... just...Well, you know... sheltering here," we heard from the window.

"Which paranormal being did you shelter from?" I teased him.

"We're sheltering here from the rain," a more confident voice sounded from another corner of the room.

"Did you run away from home?" I stated more than asked.

"No, we're just... for no reason."

"We were baking potatoes here," said a loud voice from the corner and asked, "Do you want some?"

"Come here, caterers. Don't you be afraid of us; let's face it, we are fed up with adults, not with kids."

"We're not afraid, we just... well, kinda..." the second voice objected, carefully approaching us. "It was just we were stupefied a trifle."

"That's what we thought. You chickened out a little bit and made a run partially." I hardly restrained my laughter. "So what are your names, runners?"

"I am Vital, and he's Red." A figure from the far corner started to take shape.

The boys approached the fire with one step, and I could observe them attentively. They were very young, looking no more than thirteen, their faces soiled with soot, and what was most surprising, they both had red hair. That feature made them look even more comic.

"What are you laughing at?" Vital muttered.

"It's just... kinda... just..." I imitated him. "Why are you called Vital, and he's Red? You are both red, aren't you?"

"No, I'm a little bit red," he pointed his finger at his friend and added, "but he is Red, completely red. So that's why I am Vital. Would you like some potatoes?"

"Well, cooks, we're not going to refuse a treat," we said very friendly and approached the fire.

Those kids dexterously took potatoes out of cinders and honestly divided them equally between everyone. Baked potatoes with ashes on them were incredibly tasty and extremely hot.

"All right, could you be so sweet as to tell us what you were actually doing here?" I asked.

"Wanted to bump each other off," Red answered defiantly, "but Vital won the coin toss, and this is unfair."

"If so, why were you baking potatoes?" you inquired.

"Whoever does away with himself on an empty stomach?" Red inquired, indignantly.

"We realized that life is shitty, so we decided it would be better to die, and doing this together is not so scary," Vital admitted sincerely. "Red gets beaten at school quite often, and my mom and dad bloody well fight with each other nearly every day!"

"Perhaps it sounds trite, but some days are just bad days! However, you've got to have more weighty reasons to die, and

I think you don't have any." For some reason I was amused by their story while at the same time there was nothing amusing in their statements.

"And what are you doing here?" Vital wondered, champing very loudly.

"We live here," I confessed honestly.

"Wow! Isn't it scary?" Red got surprised.

"Of course it is. That's why we are always together," you broke into laughter, "like teeth and a tongue in the same chamber."

"It's rumored that this house is haunted," Vital stepped right into the conversation. "Have you seen any ghosts here?"

"Sometimes we see them, but we've got used to them and even attached to them," you answered ironically.

At this very moment, somewhere up above, a branch of a tree started knocking on a window frame. Everybody stopped eating potatoes and listened.

"What is it?" Red asked, alarmed.

"Don't you know? It's the black hand." I suddenly remembered a scary story we used to tell in the dark, one we'd heard often enough in the foster home.

"What black hand?" Vital almost squeaked.

"It happened quite recently, or, maybe, long ago. Once upon a time there was a very docile girl; in the evenings, obeying her parents, she always went to bed in her small room until one evening, a branch knocked on the window of her room. She told her father about it; he went to break the branch and got lost. She told her mother about it; her mother went to her room and got lost, too. And then the girl decided to break the branch by herself. Outside the window was a wild downpour. She reached out to open the vent pane; and when the window finally opened, she saw that it was not a branch knocking; it was a pitch-black hand. It seized the girl and choked her, cutting her off just like that. And that's the whole story. I'm sure you are not scared, are you?"

"Not at all, those are tales for children, and we are grownups," Vital defied.

"Actually, I gotta go home," Red began to hurry, peering at the window. "And the rain has just stopped."

"Mom's going to be mad if I come home late. Well, I should probably go, too."

"So you were scared, anyway," you concluded sneeringly.

"We were not, it's just my father and he's going to beat me up." Vital voiced his thoughts aloud. "I swear we are not afraid of anything."

"If it really matters, you run." I smiled amiably.

"But if you suddenly get bored and wish to try that again, you're welcome," you chopped in.

"Only one thing I beg of you," I said. "Don't approach the window."

"Especially at night," you added, "when it's raining."

But they weren't listening. They'd already jumped up, off like two bullets.

We haven't seen them since then.

After they left we sat at the smouldering fire for a long time, drying our wet clothes. Looking at the fire, I thought how often luck depends on chance. And is it fair that a small incident can totally change a person's destiny? Eventually we got up and went to our bedroom, back to old ghosts and imaginary fears.

* * *

Our life was going imperceptibly by when the last day of April came. Twilight fell over the city as we were slowly walking in the innocent rain. Our loyal blanket got soaked in cool water, but I didn't notice, hurrying to breathe in the spring and let my soul green out. While the rain was pouring down, we, inconspicuous like everyone else around us, merged with a harmonious picture of the world hidden under raincoats, jackets, covers and umbrellas. Trying to outshout the noisy rain, you unexpectedly brought up an uncomfortable topic I didn't want to discuss.

"We've been living perhaps next door to her in the same city, but have never made any attempt to see her."

I immediately understood that you were talking about our mother. Since our earliest childhood I have never stopped wondering: why did she do it? Did she have any feelings when she abandoned us? What motivated her? I couldn't manage to put myself in her place; resentment rose up in my throat and choked me like a loop at the very thought of *her reasons*. We didn't have any information about her, neither who she was nor what she did for a living; we didn't even know her name, but we always dreamed of her. I usually associated her with a heroine of labor, a great scientist or a well-known actress, because I wanted so much to be proud of her. But as far as I knew, none of these notions was true. I had always thought of our mother as a myth, as something impossible and inconceivable, as something that didn't seem to exist but nonetheless was encountered every day.

I can't describe my feelings at that moment. It is one thing to imagine her but a totally different thing to see her for real. In addition, she believed we were dead; at least that was what they had told us in the boarding school. But what if she didn't believe in our death and had been looking for us for all these years? That was the inevitable discussion – of a tale as old as time, which you started all over again.

And you know what? I just thought, "Hope, you were so eager to go to the capital just in order to find *your* mother, not ours, all for yourself; and all these hospitals and doctors were just a convenient pretext. I can't say that I blame you; I only wish I'd realized it sooner."

"You must understand, Faith, we shouldn't take offence at her," you continued speaking. "Well, let's try to be at least a little bit positive about meeting her. After all, we can't lose anything by having a positive attitude."

I remained silent, meaningfully silent.

"Do you love her at least a little bit?" you continued.

"Do I love her?" Love is an intended sacrifice for the sake of a person of like spirit and flesh. And I *would like* to feel this kind of love, but she has never merited it. But how is it possible to love a person whom we don't even know, a person who probably betrayed us at the moment of paramount importance when we were so badly in need of her? I wanted to understand what made her do so. Was it her fault, and if it was, would she be able to acknowledge her mistakes in order to get things right? And at the same time I was ferociously scared to meet her. How would she react to the fact that we were still alive?

"Anyway, we cannot find her in such a big city, so why go on about it?" I objected, trying to instill severity into my tone. "All we have is her last name."

"I don't think so," you objected. "Actually, we know her name, too. We heard Ivan Borisovich mentioning it. Don't you remember? She has an unordinary name, Lyuba[17]."

---

17   *Lyuba* is a short name for *Lyubov* which has the meaning "love" in Russian. A name with a close meaning, *Charity*, will be used hereinafter instead of *Lyubov* in order to highlight the connotation of the name.

No way! I had completely forgotten that Ivan Borisovich, the doctor at the institute of traumatology, had named her. Even when I tried to remember, I hardly managed; it seemed so long ago. How come you have never said it aloud and never mentioned it when conversing with me? And now, it turns out that our mother's name means benevolence and generosity to people as objects of her love! A unique and beautiful name! Charity! "It is one of life's cruel ironies," I thought, "that a midwife, or whoever filled in the documents, must have known our mom's name. I suppose she had a lot of fun naming us Hope and Faith! Or, on the contrary, she sympathized."

"If we put Mom's name next to our last name, we have a chance of finding her address in the telephone directory," you triumphed with dazzlingly sparkling eyes. "And she could definitely help us to get passports," you added in a tone which admitted no doubt.

A passport, the treasured document giving a person the right to a human existence! So, this word, strengthened by the determination in your voice, possessed a miraculous power at that moment; and it was this last argument that was probably decisive.

A couple of days passed. In spite of our decision, we didn't initiate a search for our mother right away. Perhaps you wished to consider everything rationally and think over your small hopes and fears again. Indeed, making a step towards a reunion was very hard, and what bothered us most was the fact that we had to appear before her in our present dejection. The decision was soaring and roaring in the air, but we didn't hurry to put it into action. Everything remained the same. We carried on standing in the walking tunnel and begging the conscientious passersby for trifles. But one day, all of a sudden, like everything else in life, from within the depths of the tunnel,

I heard the sounds of a violin. A true maestro was playing; the instrument came to life in his hands, and the divine music spread to every corner of the tunnel. I was perplexed. How had he happened to come to this pathetic lower world of faceless shadows indifferent to truth and to reality, to the sufferings of human beings? I caught myself staring at him. He was slightly hunched and round-shouldered, plainly dressed, looking about thirty-five, with a serene face, a mild smile and an old man's eyes. He put a sign on his breast with an inscription asking for help for his dying son. Then he played a waltz – vivid, breezy, spring-spirited, and absolutely incongruous. Moreover, it was impossible to raise the huge amount of money necessary for the rare and expensive surgery his son needed. He too was aware of this but still he played on, muffling the roar of his grief with music. And the greater the pain he felt, the shriller the violin sounded. He was dying very slowly, together with his son, perishing from his own powerlessness and feebleness; all in all, it resembled rather a dying agony than a musician playing. What a pity that all beautiful things are so fragile and so fleeting! Soon, two supervisors of stately proportions approached the poor man and rudely pushed him outside. I can't describe the pain I had at that moment: literally, physically, I felt his despair, this awful, inhuman torment when we cannot change anything because it is already too late. That's when I thought that finding someone to love was more important than anything else. Of course, our mother probably didn't go through the tortures suffered by that unfortunate violinist, and furthermore she didn't need us like he needed his son. But, maybe she too had felt the need to let a load off her mind over all the long years. Anticipating this, I almost saw Mother right in front of me, clothed in white, vivid and real. From that moment on, I had one irresistible desire – to look into her eyes.

Now I was anxious to see her and believed it would definitely happen.

That very day we bought a telephone directory in the book market and faced the daunting task: seven people with the sought-after names turned out to be living in the city. But what was most important was that in the directory we found addresses opposite the names. We therefore had a great opportunity to look for her from a distance at least, instead of making phone calls. That was what I thought; however, your plans were totally different and you took a decision I couldn't agree to, but was unable to change. You dragged us to a telephone booth with the quickness of our four feet. Fortunately, the only booth that was working was occupied. Activity gave way to the chance to gather our thoughts and put off an uncomfortable conversation with a person named Charity. But soon enough the booth became vacant, and you resolutely pushed us inside. Having dialed the first number from the list, we, with baited breath, started counting the beeps. After a while – which seemed like a whole, perfect eternity – we heard a female voice saying hello. A thousand questions whirled through my mind, the most important questions of my life which I wanted, planned, had to ask... but, of course, I didn't. I hung up without saying a word. You understood everything from my look of despair. What could we say to an absolutely unfamiliar lady, even if she turned out to be our mother? For good or for bad, words were meaningless and inappropriate; we needed to see her reaction to us. We had nothing but to choose the last option: to check all the addresses, knock on every door and look in the face of each and every one of those residents personally. For some reason, we had no doubt whatsoever that we would be able to recognize our own mother.

Mom, You've Got a Visitor

Next day we didn't go to work – for the first time. Instead, we started the day by searching for our mother, checking the addresses in the order they were listed in the telephone directory, from top to bottom. We headed off to the first Charity's address with mixed feelings. I was scared about what would happen if we found her because I had nothing to tell her, but you, on the other hand, were overwhelmed with impatience. I knew how desperately eager you were to see her but you should have understood: you and I were not ordinary children and we couldn't predict how our mother would react; the books didn't say anything about this. We spent two long, senseless hours in the entrance hall of one apartment building, that's how long it took you to force me to walk upstairs. The first half of the morning had already passed, and our would-be mother could have left for work long ago, walked by accidentally and not even recognized us.

At last I gained courage and we rang the doorbell. In the silence we heard an electric canary singing, the door opened, and a tall and extremely skinny young man of about our age, with long hair, almost feminine features and a thin aquiline nose appeared before us. Nobody said a word; he studied us attentively – we had left our blanket at home - and we looked at him vacantly. However, our appearance was not particularly surprising to him; on the contrary, it evoked genuine interest.

"Can I help you?" he asked in an absolutely harmless voice.

"Excuse me, does Ms. Charity live here?" you asked, in a faltering voice.

The young man measured us with another glance of limitless curiosity and then called into the depths of the apartment:

"Mom, mummy, you've got a visitor."

She has a son! It turns out that if this woman is our mother, then he must be our brother. It was scary to think about, but a flash of hope emerged. Soon, a rather stout woman with a puffy face and a brush-haircut appeared on the staircase. Despite her gloomy looks, a strange and incomprehensible warmth enveloped us when she appeared, and at that very moment I thought how great it would be if she turned out to be our mother.

She peered into our faces for a long while, but couldn't stop worrying.

"Can I help you?" She repeated her son's question.

Didn't recognize or didn't want to? Her eyes spoke for her: neither sudden fright, nor pleasure, nor happiness were reflected in them, only bewilderment. *This is not her!* No doubt about it. At that very moment, we wished to disappear, vanish into thin air, or even better, become invisible, quietly creep into the room after her and live there for a while, carelessly pretending we were staying at home with our family. But instead we had to whisper, "Sorry, there must be some mistake…" and immediately go downstairs. Once again we stood in the entrance hall for a long time, experiencing a new feeling, sudden like rain, wanting to hide in some hole and never leave. We seemed to become even more miserable than before.

Our next "mother" was a very old, weak-sighted woman near ninety. She tried to see if she recognized who we were but couldn't see us properly. However, we saw her quite well. After the traditional question, "Can I help you?" and receiving no answer, she re-entered the darkness of the corridor, probably wanting to fetch her glasses or to ask for help, but when she or they returned there was already no sign of us.

We had a lengthy dispute about whether we should check the remaining five addresses or forget everything and go back to our regular life. We didn't think that our mother could have a family or that we could have a brother or a sister. Are they going to accept us as we are? But you persistently stood your ground. "I want to look this bitch in the face; I have a right to be somebody's child!" you shouted, experiencing an unexpected change of heart and not even admitting the possibility of being unsuccessful in our search. But success was questionable. Would we get lucky and find her in that big city with only a list of names as our guide and helpmate? Eventually, your hatred – that had emerged like sharp teeth – and my growing curiosity made us get on with our "mission".

The third "mother" died a few years ago; at least that's what we were told through a closed door.

The next two were very young women, a bit older than us, and so everything was much easier. We just turned around and left, and they, shrugging their shoulders, dispassionately closed their doors on us and immediately forgot about our existence.

The door of the sixth apartment had an improper word inscribed on it in chalk. First, we rang the doorbell but there was no sound of ringing; a little while later we knocked timidly. After a minute, we heard footsteps, then the door opened wide, letting out kitchen smells onto a bare staircase, and we saw a sleepy woman's face. Perhaps in the past she had been pretty, but now, under her dressing gown, we could imagine her bloated body and, indeed, saw its outlines. Her hair was gathered into a messy knot and her face revealed excessive suspicion and discontent.

"What do you want?" she asked very rudely and mistrustfully.

"Sorry, it must be a mistake," you mumbled contritely.

We will never recognize our real mother! We rushed away and were already going downstairs not even daring to look back when we heard a loud "wait". Jumping down steps, the woman hurried after us. The expression on her face had drastically changed. Annoyance was replaced by excitement; her manner became more serious and almost ingratiating. Probably, not knowing the best way to start, she rumpled and crumpled her fingers, cracking their joints for a while before opening with:

"So, you are my...?" her face reddened, but her voice was unnaturally calm, almost indifferent.

"My... who?" you reacted severely.

"My... my... daughters," she said in a trembling voice and tears welled up in her eyes. She was just like the Bollywood actresses on old posters we used to see every so often.

"Yes, we are," I heard your strangled voice; however, your lips were squeezed tightly together, and your answer sounded a little unnatural, as if you spoke through a keyhole, but the woman for some reason peered into my face insinuatingly. I grew cold. I had to answer; that "yes" was mine!

"Come into my place," she said with a shade of solemnity, and not waiting for our reply, she went forward.

We obediently followed her into the depths of an endless corridor which looked like a very narrow tunnel. I believe that you cried. As for our mother, we didn't surprise her or frighten her; she was self-possessed and calm, as if she had been preparing for this moment all her life. I must admit, I expected something more from that first meeting... and while we were walking, I kept my eyes down, trying not to think a lot, and not to fall, but once we had entered a spacious, clean, almost sterile room, the scene of our family reunion began.

"My girls, I am so glad that you are alive, so happy I found you," our mother started lamenting. In her voice, grief mixed with overwhelming joy and appeasement. "How long has your journey been?"

I wanted to jump up and say: "Twenty years, even more!" but I contained myself. You were speechless with excitement, and mother continued speaking to both of us:

"You must be scared of me."

We shook our heads immediately.

"Maybe you think I am a madwoman? Just look how many mentally unstable people are around us these days and *then* you will understand who is normal. A woman living next door to my bathroom always pries into other people's affairs and obviously mine, pins her ear to my wall, and wants to oust me and take my room. Why did you say hello to her?" She addressed me with the look of a person tired of injustice.

I had only said "hello" to some woman, gray and dried up like a mummy, as we passed by the kitchen, so I didn't know how to react to mother's remark. Probably, that mummy-neighbor, by chance, had become a witness to our long-awaited meeting. We probably looked completely dejected. Though it was true that our mother was there, in front of us, we still didn't know how to react. At last she hugged and kissed us, but, as if startled, immediately went into a corner of the room and started setting up a large extension table. She turned away and spoke over her shoulder, grunting:

"The first day after the delivery they said you were dead, but I didn't believe them and started searching for you, but wherever I went, I faced the same dreadful situation: everybody was silent; nobody said anything. Nevertheless, I had a feeling that you were alive. And I kept searching on and on. I waited for you every day. So many tears I shed at night. Oh, so many. Because of it, my hair turned gray before its time and I lost my good looks. Who is going to take interest in me now? That's why your father left me; he's a rascal, if ever I saw one. Is there anybody on earth who can love him more than I did? What a fool he was; he made it worse for himself. After all, it was him who signed the surrender."

She kept on talking and talking, halting and contradicting her own words, and we stood there riveted to the spot, listening and not knowing what to say, or do. Should we help her lay out the cups or find a suitable way to step aside and not get in her way?

We might have stood there forever but suddenly mother stopped talking. Not finishing her sentence, she turned away to the window and started crying quietly.

As time went on, I began to be gnawed by doubts. Was she just acting, or was I suspicious of her for no good reason?

"Last night I had a nightmare that I was dying," Mother started talking again, in a voice full of drama. "Air, I need air, I am suffocating," and she squeezed her neck with her hand as if it was occurring there and then. "I'm trying to shout but I can't make a sound. I'm trying to move but I can't budge. I want to call for help, but there is nobody around. I am all alone. My God, how horrible it was! I was so frightened, terrified! So what would happen if I really died? I can't imagine what you would do without your poor mother who loves you so much."

"Well, sure, we couldn't do without her," I quipped in my mind. "We would be dead for another twenty-something years!"

"Don't worry, now we are going to take care of you," you tried to calm her down and make her listen. Your voice was trembling; I couldn't believe my ears. Where did all your anger go to?

"I can't tell you how glad I am you came," our mother almost sang out, and, like a conjurer, produced an old watch literally out of nowhere.

"Here! This is your father's watch. For merits," she said with anguish, putting it on your wrist. "You know who granted it to him? This... well... what was that villain's name... he honored him!"

The more I listened, the less I believed a single word, a single teardrop flowing down her face, her face powdered so heavily it looked like an abstract mask. She doesn't love us and she never did. She abandoned us because she wanted to. It was her choice. But you, you gave credence to her and thereby suffered together with her; you were so glad to meet Mother! And all this incongruity between your great expectations and reality probably seemed to you a small fee for the long-awaited happiness.

Instead of celebrating and rejoicing at our family reunion – telling stories, sharing impressions, laughing – we were sitting at a laid table, having tea, with terrifying composure. Just imagine, after so many years of separation, we were simply drinking tea as if we had been doing this daily for hundreds of years, having long ago exhausted all subjects of conversation, except one, obviously our mother's favorite. At great length, exhaustively, Mother enjoyed telling us about herself, rarely asking questions and answering them by herself. She believed that all people were rascals and swindlers. In her hatred she had neither pity nor mercy, and a large number of her curses and unflattering reviews were dedicated to her feckless neighbors and to our father who had dared to offend her and then abandon her. She ignored our questions, withdrawing into herself or looking for an imaginary spoon fallen under the table.

After asking our names, she nearly had a heart attack, reminding me of a stranded fish intermittently opening and closing its mouth. By a miraculous coincidence, Hope and Faith were the names she had dreamt of giving her daughters if ever she'd had *normal* ones.

"Just think of it, I've never had any serious diseases. Why were you born that way?" and she immediately started answering herself. "There is no answer. Congenital deformity is one of life's deepest mysteries."

But I knew the answer. A person like her could only produce freaks. Nothing normal could grow in her womb. We are the reflections of her human nature, symbols, deformed symbols, of her view of life.

Tea had cooled down long ago when a second neighbor peeped into the room. First of all, from behind the door appeared an examining lonely eye, then we saw a sniffing nose and then the whole head squeezed into the aperture.

"Here you are! Gennady Karlovich," Mother exclaimed happily. "Come, come in!" she added impatiently.

This neighbor's face, perfectly round like a pancake, finally responded to the invitation and expressed the kindest smile. Soon Gennady Karlovich Kucheryavy[18] entirely filtered through the doorway, squeezed in as if by miracle. He resembled a huge hog with small piggy eyes, faded eyelashes and rusty hair. Hardly had he appeared before Mother underwent the most improbable, the most unnatural change. Her face lit up like a

---

18   Kucheryavy in Russian means "curly"; in slang dodge, agile - a person who is able to be well settled in life.

candle-light at dinner, and she started mumbling something indistinctly, driven either by pleasure or by confusion. Furthermore, once he threw an eye on the refrigerator, she immediately sprang to her feet and began to take out sausage, beet salad and sprats.

"And these are my... come, come, sit down," mother joyfully muttered. "Just my... well, you know."

Actually, Gennady Karlovich didn't, and wasn't going to; lazily, almost unwillingly he took a seat on two chairs simultaneously, while we were huddling on one with difficulty, and quietly farted.

"Hope and Faith," mother squeezed out urgently. "And this is Gennady Karlovich. He is such a wonderful person, unlike those menials." And having waved her hand towards the door, she put newly-baked pasties on the table.

"Oh, how pretty they are!" he muttered cryptically, giving us a playful wink, and the sweetest smile spread all over his face.

"Come on, children, eat well!" and taking a look at us, Mother gave a tragic sigh. "You must be hungry."

Frankly speaking, we hadn't eaten anything since morning, our stomachs were knotted with hunger, and our heads went round giddily. But Gennady Karlovich had probably "fasted"[19] much longer than us. He was eating in such a manner as if he had been starved of food all his life, stopping only to smooth his scanty hair or to pinch the fur on his chest. His entire organism seemed to consist only of a stomach taking up the biggest part of his jellylike body; he didn't even chew his food but like an ogre swallowed it whole. I stared at him with barely disguised

---

19   A temporary abstention from taking meals and drinking is referred to here.

horror but mother was foolish with adoration. He started on the pasties and didn't stop until only one remained on the plate – probably, that was his particular expression of courtesy, of generosity. He then proceeded to devour the sausage with beet salad and sprats, having seasoned them with two bowls of soup, and, for "dessert", he finished off the remaining "courtesy" pasty. He was a gourmet, he informed us, not a glutton.

Gennady possessed a picturesque appearance. Pink bald spots were already outlined on his head, making him attempt to disguise them by combing his hair sideways; his fingers with bitten nails resembled short, thick sausages. He never washed himself as a matter of principle, considering washing in water an absolute waste of time. In his leisure time, he liked to look through personal advertisements in newspapers, reminding me of a mangy tomcat ready for action at the sight of any young woman's body. Probably, for this reason, he treated our mother very frostily but openly flirted with us, trying to make gags and telling obscene, true-life stories and gross jokes every now and again.

Somehow there was only one time when our mother entered into the conversation. Having heard hardly distinguishable singing behind the wall, she only said through her teeth, either mockingly or with excitement:

"People started singing. That's all from desperation."

At half past ten Gennady Karlovich got up from the table and, without even saying goodbye, made his way to the door; however, at the threshold he stopped and, after thinking a while, uttered:

"Well, you must come round to my place for a while. It'll be so nice to see you both."

He had hardly gone out before Mother, piercing us with a scathing look, hissed querulously:

"Did nobody teach you at school that you should hold a knife in your right hand, and scoop the soup from the front of the bowl to the back!?"

We listened to her submissively and ashamedly, being used to obeying the orders of elders. It is much easier to forgive and forget than to be obstinate and resist. Eventually, having finished savoring her absolute domination over us, she indulgently made us a bed – a real bed with real bed linen – then coldly and a little fastidiously stroked only you briefly on the head and went to sleep.

"She didn't even ask where we came from today," I whispered with disappointment. "Where we live."

"Who cares, if we're living at her place from now on," you cut in rationalizing, and started snoring demonstratively. I'm sure if you only could have, you would have turned over on the other side.

Late night shrouded the city; a pregnant moon was sliding across the dome of the sky. My troubled sleep was interrupted by a shrill squeak of springs. I opened my eyes and saw Mother sitting on the corner of our bed and watching me very closely. Her moonlit face expressed a surprising humility and fondness as though her true, maternal essence, patient and caring, was just now showing itself while the other, false, hysterical and suspicious, was sleeping undisturbed on the couch, snoring and snuffling quietly. I wanted to shake you awake and tell you everything would be okay, but mother pressed her finger to her lips, silently asking me not to do so, then she put her hand on my head and carefully stroked my hair as if I were a child. That very moment, as if by magic, I forgave her all her sins, offences and wrongdoings, and soon fell asleep deeply and serenely. When I woke up, the dawn had already broken behind the window; Mother was still sleeping and some doubts started rising in my mind. Was that really her or was that one of my dreams last night with her in it?

The next week we took great pains to help her about the house, went grocery shopping and spent our own money on food; and mother, as she saw us paying, scolded us for unreasonable extravagance and inability to be tight with money. Finally, we decided to give her our scarce savings on moral grounds. Meanwhile, Gennady Karlovich acquired the unchangeable status of a frequent guest in our humble dwelling; working as a taxi driver only at nights and returning home at daybreak, he had all his meals at our place, always cheered our mother up, kept boosting her morale. But when he paid a bit more attention to us, at that very moment she grew gloomy and silent. Gennady, however, didn't bother about these changes in her moods, continuing to emit an inexhaustible stream of vulgar nonsense in which he had no equal.

All our life we had been dreaming of getting through every little hole in order to enter this beautiful and unfamiliar world where parents and children love each other, not to get anything but to spite everything, where love is all-important, to plunge into a "true" fairy-tale world, to settle down and live happily ever after. So why didn't I feel happy when it was happening for real? I realized that everything seemed to be fine but my soul, with tearful eyes, did not believe in what was happening. I just couldn't embrace a huge discrepancy between the way I watched Mother every day and the way she appeared before me that very first night. An obvious trap was concealed in all this. Mother reminded me of a dark storeroom with numerous boxes full of old things; we go inside and move ahead into the depths, trying not to touch anything, and as long as we do it, everything goes well, but a single wrong step suffices for the burden of the past to collapse and to bury us alive.

Several times a day, repeating herself and getting confused, Mother told us the story of her life, full of immense hopes and dramatic disappointments. Her dream was to become a great actress, and it came true, which is not a particularly common thing but a reason for pride. However, she didn't become a great actress, but a minor, restricted one. In the theater she faced certain troubles from the very beginning. Somebody always wanted to take her place or oppressed her or never let her play leading roles. And all this happened despite her creativity and her rich inner world. She deemed all theater directors, without exception, to have no talent, but most often her anger was directed against actresses. She couldn't stand competition from anybody in any form, neither at work, nor in her private life. She was blessed with good looks but deprived of talent. At work, she always overacted, and to protect herself, she was only able to swear and push people around. Boldly claiming directors lacked professional skill, she switched from one theater to another until nobody wanted to work with her. She came to be a total fiasco. In general, all her employment and relationship stories ended up with angry lamentations and curses, which "proved" that she was totally surrounded by enemies or bastards. And every time, after "turning her soul inside out", she could be seen, nervously smoking near the window, having a good, long cry, calming down till her next outburst. Used to boredom and monotony, we spent a whole week together: quiet Faith, passionate Hope and illusory Charity. Unimaginable that some families can spend all their lives thus!

* * *

One morning Gennady Karlovich came in, which wasn't particularly surprising. Occasionally glancing at us and smiling greasily, he had a long and agitated conversation with Mother. Once he left, she gave us a towel and new toothbrushes, which were considered a luxury, and sent us to the bathroom, being especially sweet and caring. You were overwhelmed with joy, and while we were taking a shower, you tried to appeal to my conscience in an undertone: "It's not our mother who should take care of us; it's us who should take care of her from now on." After our shower we drank tea again, which was beginning to make me feel sick.

"And now, listen," Mother said imperatively, breaking the silence, "our Gennady Karlovich is a very lonely person and *definitely* needs some help. I want you to go to his room right now".

And loudly, as if to overcome our objections (which actually never came), she continued impatiently:

"I don't want to listen to anything. Do go!" and started taking the dishes off the table.

Once we entered Gennady's room, mother slammed the door behind us. We found him half-naked. I remember noticing a surprising disproportion between his massive body and his very thin, short legs. Furthermore, for the sake of completeness, his red, bearlike fur, as if torn out of him on purpose, was scattered all over the place: on the chairs, on window sills, on the couch; we could even see it between magazines and newspapers, mixed up with dust. Gennady stood in the middle of the room and shivered either from cold or impatience, smiling oilily. The entire room became permeated with the smell of his sweat, which seemed to be emitted even by the furniture.

"What guests have come to honor my humble home?" he said, ingratiatingly. "Come here. And stop huddling together like penguins. Don't be afraid. I won't bite you." He burst out laughing. "Well, as you wish. I'm almost ready, anyway. Now it's your turn to get undressed."

An absolute, almost hostile silence reigned in the room. I saw what he was driving at and started to inspect the room in search of heavy objects. Meanwhile, you began to pull off your sweater, then your t-shirt. It seemed like we stood on opposite sides of a barricade. I stiffened, watching the situation as if from the sidelines, and felt the changes occurring inside you. You were being transformed into a complete stranger which for me was very dangerous, crossing an invisible line which guarded our safety. Till at last, it hit me that the former Hope didn't exist anymore; she would not be coming back and we could never shake off the painful memories of what was happening by just shrugging our shoulders.

I felt this weird wave of nausea in my throat, but not in my stomach. I was ashamed. I abhorred our lousy situation. Undressing, you bared both of us, and I stood like an impersonal being or the narrator of a story, not knowing how to distance myself from your performance. Unable any longer to observe the scene, I closed my eyes tightly, not from fear, but from shame. The oppressive silence around me was accompanied by darkness. The whole world had stopped, frozen in indecision. I was powerless. And at that very moment, all of a sudden your voice broke the stinking, suffocating, unreal silence like a sewer pipe.

"What are you staring at, you idiot? Just do something. But don't touch the sister."

That very cynical statement you made was filled with chilling tranquility; like a cold shower, it opened my eyes. Everything remained pretty much the same. Gennady stood in the same place and resembled a shaggy, rusted monument rather than a living person. We were still side by side; however, something had changed irrevocably. He no longer had control over the situation; now you were the one giving orders.

"Pick up your jaw from the floor. Look, what a freaking good surprise you got!" Your voice "encouraged" him mockingly.

Gennady didn't say a word, nervously running his fingers over his baggy underpants and blinked uncontrollably.

"You don't want me anymore? What's the matter? Shit or get off the pot!" You threw hurtful words at him with great force, and our body started shuddering with frantic laughter.

"That's because I'm tired," Gennady mumbled plaintively, "I've been working all night. I'll be all right tomorrow. Promise I will."

"If you're so tired, go to sleep, you impotent, fat fool!" you mocked, putting on your sweater.

I must admit, I got frightened, expecting an uncontrollable reaction from that Russian half-bear, half-hog, so can you imagine how surprised I was when he confusedly and even childishly started to persuade us not to tell Mother about the incident, not to tell anyone?!

"There's nothing to tell, because you couldn't do anything," you hissed sarcastically, rubbing salt in the wound.

"But I am still going to pay her, as if everything went well," he was mumbling and growing red to match the color of his body-hair. It turned out that he was afraid of mockery like everybody else. And then slowly, hardly moving disobedient feet, he sat down on the chair nearby and started crying.

"What was about him that made him so special and could attract our mother?" I thought, looking at his endless tears. "Was it about his patronymic[20] giving an illusive hint to his

---

20   The patronymic *Karlovich* derives from *Karl*, a popular German name.

German roots, or was it just a trivial physiological need, the most pressing issue for a woman who was already growing old?" For me, it remained a riddle. Only one thing was obvious. Our mother had planned Gennady's "little discomfiture" in advance. Her hatred towards us was stronger than her love for him. How strange that was. Charity, who was supposed to be at least a slight bit benevolent, merciful and charitable, took revenge because "someone else" was preferred to her. But there again she took revenge on everybody, even herself.

And she succeeded in her revenge wonderfully well. Gennady Karlovich was sobbing like a child. Though I didn't have much sympathy for him, with my heart I understood how bad he felt and wished to speak a comforting word. But you, on the contrary, were full of contempt and hatred; that new image of you was the absolute copy of our mother's character, her flesh and blood.

"Ok, enough chewing the rag! C'mon, ante up!" you ordered, enforcing your power over him. "We're supposed to get your pay, not her."

Poor Gennady Karlovich, totally confused, started taking out his wallet, and at that very moment Mother broke into the room; probably she had been listening behind closed doors to our entire conversation.

"Oh, you fucking little wretches! Have you decided to rob your poor mother? You aren't a bit better than your father, you ungrateful, filthy bastards!"

"I won't give you money," separating one word from another, you muttered. "I *honestly* earned it."

"You're lying, you piece of junk!" and she suddenly rushed at us, craning her neck and popping her eyes out. "Whoever's going to lay eyes on you, lame thing? I should've choked you to death in the maternity hospital."

Her heavy, black words were pressing like pig-iron kettle-bells, and she hurriedly spat them out as though she was afraid to suffocate. I was intolerably ashamed for her, not for us. Meanwhile, she started shaking your hand to tear off the watch she had gifted you, and continued yelling in a heart-rending voice:

"I haven't seen you for years, and now you appear out of nowhere. You want my apartment, don't you? Well, bite me!" and she made an obscene gesture right in front of my face. "Whoever invited you here? Do you think it is easy to be a mother of such freaks?" she shouted across the crowd of faces that had started to gather in a lopsided doorway next to us.

Oh, this tormenting concern that your neighbor's life might be better than yours! And how great it feels when you realize that the truth is exactly the opposite; and we're not so different after all. Nothing brings true neighbors together like *a little friendly competition.*

It seemed that our mother could elicit exceptional critical praise and wild ovations from the public any moment she liked. You shivered, but didn't protest, and she didn't yell any more but croaked, flooded with damnations:

"Help me, people! I've been robbed! I wish you were dead, you bitches!"

Her face got black with rage, her legs gave way under her and she fell down and started rolling on the floor, belching out absurd pleadings and disgraceful curses.

"Hate you. I hate this *thing* I gave birth to. Filthy creeps, ghouls."

I was overcome by extreme disgust; you were limp and pale as chalk. As for Gennady Karlovich, he was the only one impassively watching the scene, like a passerby who has gotten involved in a theatrical performance by mistake. In addition, he managed to keep the money to himself.

The final moments of this monumental, epic story dissolved into the most trivial of farces. The neighbors who had gathered in the corridor to look at us were covering their giggling faces with their hands and loudly whispering, exchanging their opinions on Ms. Charity's behavior that had already become a habit, and her conjoined, two-headed monster that had dishonored the principal tenant G. K. Kucheryavy. Their faces were shining with joy and tenderness, they were happy: now talking and reminiscing would suffice and lift up, however temporarily, their miserable, cheerless lives. Meanwhile, our mother kept coiling and jerking her feet restlessly.

"Let's get out of here," you said dispiritedly. "It's no use searching in a place where there is nothing."

And the pain of frustrated hope and broken faith sounded so clearly and openly in your words that all those who were present, including G. K. K., felt uncomfortable and fell silent.

"Come now, please," you repeated, feeling that your dreams were the opposite of reality.

As we approached the door, we stopped and looked back. Neighbors, who had assembled like relatives ready to shoot a family portrait, watched us closely, with great concentration, but we didn't care anymore. We stepped across the threshold, determined never to return. The door-lock clicked behind our backs and echoed, bouncing off the walls, doubled, then trebled that sound as though all the doors of the world were closing one by one, and the unflattering truth was eventually showing itself. "From here on you go alone, forever forsaken, forever alone."

Armless Tsar

Strange thoughts visit me sometimes. Was it exactly as I remember, or did you see everything in a different light? And can it be that I greatly exaggerate all human imperfections, highlighting our ugly duckling burdens? Hardened in heart and having no other weapon but my own suffering, could I exhort others to do things they otherwise would not do? What if I were secretly in love with my failures and wished them to continue forever?

All the way "home" I was looking for an opportunity to discuss the Mother story with you, but you just kept wincing and turning away, awkwardly stumbling now and again. Try as I might, I couldn't find the right words to talk about the incident. We eventually arrived at our abandoned house. I felt more unwanted than unhappy, as if we had been brought into the world and then expelled from it. I held no grudge against my mother. I forgave her. But was my forgiveness sincere? Is it possible to forgive a traitor without perceiving the true reasons for his or her treachery? Is it another lie intended to justify all previous lies? I would really like to know what you think about the bullshit, this bullshit, my bullshit. However, I often seem to understand you better when you are asleep!

The following day, driven by necessity ("We have to go back," you agreed, "or else we'll kick the bucket…"), we returned to the tunnel. However, even the obvious need for money faded by comparison with our growing impatience to plunge into the living, swarming mass again, to disappear completely. It was irresistible, like the urge to sneeze. I couldn't live anymore without this chaotic, overflowing stream sliding through the tunnel like a well-trained but confused animal. I thought if we disappeared at least for a moment, so that nobody would notice us, pointing their fingers and making fun of us, I would not go crazy. Attention of any kind was also better than no attention at all. And at the same time the tunnel was the best place on earth for us to hide, to take a breather. You see how confused I felt!

Life in the tunnel hadn't changed; everything remained in *the right* place. Same as before, all the sundry people hurried somewhere, indifferently, listlessly, same as before. We were met with "open arms", so to speak.

"Well, look who decided to show up!" the supervisor shouted gleefully. "Hydra returned, by itself, on its own four feet."

"Is our spot still waiting for us?" you inquired in a matter-of-fact way.

"You don't even know what is waiting for you, two-headed freak," the pug muttered with muffled rage. "I will cure you of your habit of leaving without permission."

After that he grabbed you, seized you by the throat and shook you with such force that even my teeth clanked, and the last coins fell out of our pockets.

"Take your hands off me, jackass," you croaked, barely able to catch your breath.

It happened in a flash. Next moment the pug hit you with all his strength. Suddenly the earth turned upside down; both of us dropped on the floor and all the noises around us quieted down. In the dead silence, somewhere far away, I heard his voice:

"Pray, bitch!" and he gobbed generous spittle on us, completing our humiliation.

Who could think that the ceiling and the walls of the tunnel could look so alike! I lay motionless, feeling neither pain, nor fear, most probably just the fear of pain. "I'd better not rise; it is safer," I thought with bitter pleasure.

"I will pray for the repose of his soul," you hissed, choking with fury now. "Let him burn in hell!"

And while we were slowly getting up, rubbing our hurt sides and hands, you repeated many times: "I wish him dead, scumbag. I wish him dead".

"You have to run away from here," a barely audible, unfamiliar voice rustled somewhere nearby.

Turning, we saw a skinny, almost invisible, armless little man. Resembling a broom or a mop, he stood as if glued to the nearby dirty wall.

Having spat out blood, you said loudly, "I won't go anywhere." And I nodded curtly, "We don't have anywhere to go." So we approached the mop "neighbor" to hear him better.

"He will either cripple you with his own hands or hire someone else to cripple you," the armless man said, and suddenly burst out laughing heartrendingly. His laughter was so bewitching that I didn't get all his irony immediately. To cripple *the cripples*, that was really ridiculous.

"I've been standing here for a long time, much longer than you," his voice sounded conspiratorial, "and realized years ago that they beat the armless people not because we are repulsive freaks but because we can't hit back," and again, he couldn't stop his feverish laughter mixed equally with despair and rage. "If both of you only knew how I hate them. I hate them all. Those who pass by, those who donate alms, those who take away the earnings – *I hate you all!*" he almost barked out the last words, not talking to us anymore. "A-ah, let it all go to hell. Come on, move on your way," he addressed the passersby.

"Keep on ignoring me. Of course, you are right. I'm a nonentity. Yes, I can lick your shoes, but you are still going to step on my arms. Oh, and by the way, I don't have any arms. See?" and, having waved his invisible arms, he broke into uncontrollable shrieks of laughter yet again. "And if I only had them, I would strangle all of you; each and every one of you."

"The armless tsar," I thought to myself. However, if he really had arms and power, or just the arms, *most probably* he would have spoken differently!

The poor guy continued to express his thoughts aloud to the passersby, but we didn't hear him anymore; only chaotic roars scattered along the tunnel. I stood thinking. Was the absence of arms the true reason for his hatred or was it hatred itself dwelling in his heart inherently and giving sense to his life? He seemed to cherish the hate as a source of strength to live on forever.

"I wish he would die, nitwit," in tune with the armless, you hissed discontentedly. "I won't let him even lay a finger on us."

"What finger? He has no arms at all." I was puzzled, but I immediately realized what the issue was.

"I'm not talking about this gimpy one. I'm talking about the pug who decided to teach us a lesson. Clear? He won't take me unawares again."

And, frowning angrily, you snatched a screwdriver from your pocket, drawing it forth like a sword from a sheath.

"Have you really lost your mind? Where did you get that from?" I could hardly breathe. Astonishment stopped my breath.

"We need it more than *she* does," you snarled, "and don't give me that look! You know who I'm talking about."

Did she steal it from Mother? I'd already quit being surprised, but tell me – I have always wanted to know.

"I took her lipstick, too," you grinned. "Don't panic, I'll take care of us. Not a single bitch can hurt us now. Whosoever is hard is going to find it hard to keep his own life. That one especially. I wish he was already dead. The bastard!"

Unfortunately, you were right again. We had no choice but to defend ourselves. Isn't that what wild animals do? But I am not an animal, though nobody treats me as a human. I'm just a stupid girl: silly, naive, blind. I have been hiding under the blanket for so long that I have finally lost all connection to reality; I flattered the world in hope of flattery in return. Perhaps, it's just the way I am – I can dispense with everything in this life, but I can never dispense with hope.

Driven by emotional despair, I began to hug you and started crying… and people flashed past us: half-lonely, half-unhappy, half-resigned, half-alive, giving us occasional, stealthy looks, full of pity and contempt.

"Who is that over there?" you blurted out, poking me in the side. "Look."

Having brushed away my tears and thoughts, I looked in the direction you pointed in and saw someone's head peeping out from behind a distant column. Having met my eyes, the head hid at once; however, a few moments later, a strange, rounded shadow separated itself cautiously from the wall and started walking away, breaking into a run at the exit of the tunnel.

"I see *it* for the first time," I answered quietly.

"So do I." You shrugged your shoulders. "Probably, our pug-bastard sent someone to *kill us*. Don't you think this is strange?"

You're asking! Actually, everything seemed strange to me that day. How fast-changing is our world! While we holed up at our mother's, human society, remaining the same in appearance, changed at its core, reminding me of a broken clock which seemed to be still working, but already showed the wrong time. Meanwhile, the same figure approached us from the opposite direction.

"He's going round in circles!" you exclaimed, putting your hand in your pocket.

Stooping a little and bending his knees, an impossible person, similar to a flat pumpkin rolling along the rough road, came nearer to us. He walked lopsidedly; it seemed as if he might split up and fall over at any moment. He was dressed in an old, well-used suit, very tight trousers and a carelessly knotted tie with dark green threads sticking out from the fabric. A couple of steps from us, he stopped abruptly, doubtful whether he should come closer, silently faltered and then hesitated for a while as if trying to understand his own thoughts. He had a silly, ridiculous look on his face, but for some reason I hoped to hear a revelation from him. A small, bald spot shone on the top of his head, his face-skin was flaking, eyes bulging. He was shaking with fear or shyness. To make matters worse, he had small, babyish fingers with long, dirty nails and his white, lifeless hands looked – especially in the tunnel lighting – as if dusted with flour. I could have counted to one hundred twice before he managed to regain his self-composure. Having moved a little closer, he got up on tiptoe to be on a level with our height, and once he opened his mouth, you lost your temper:

"If you wish to give alms, well, drop it or go away."

He gave us a surprised look as though he had just remembered where he was, smiled foolishly and finally squeezed out a few words:

"I'm sorry but I'm going to walk away. Don't take offence, please."

"We're not easily offended," you growled. "So what do you want?"

"You reminded me of the babe I used to know and, so to speak, reopened a wound in my soul..."

His sugary, ingratiating voice enshrouded us like dough.

"Do you wanna blame us for your reopened wound!" you exclaimed with a cold sneer and then whispered to me casually, "This is another insane guy just for us!"

"I am not insane, I'm just deeply unhappy," he moaned plaintively, hearing your words; meanwhile, the smell of sour flesh coming from his mouth struck our faces. We had to hold our breath and turn away.

"If you could only imagine..." he whimpered, almost sighing, and then faltered again, evidently not knowing how to finish the phrase.

However, we didn't get to know what would happen if "we could only imagine".

"Look, can you get us some vodka?" you interrupted him sharply. "I'm terribly thirsty."

The pumpkin-shaped stranger didn't pay much attention to your question – at least not right away – and pulled out an infernally dirty, almost stiffened handkerchief from his pocket, and started blowing his nose.

"What a *wonderful way* to ignore inconvenient questions," I thought grinning, and at this very moment a wild, inhuman yell sounded nearby.

Having woken up from their daily cares and getting caught up in a faceless stream of strangers behind changing masks, people clumsily hurried in the direction of the shouting. Driven by a weird and inexplicable impulse, we rushed after the passersby, and, having squeezed tightly in between them, froze to the spot. In front of us, lost in unknown reverie, the supervisor was sitting on the dirty floor and blinking much faster than normal. His chest was heaving with rapid breath, his lips were whistling, and were it not for an open wound in his neck, you might think he was resting or playing the fool. I stared at the pug clinging to life and didn't feel anything: neither hatred, nor pity. Nothing. And his ripped throat kindly smiled at me, drooling bloody saliva and whispering: "Pray, bitches, you will all be punished by death."

Meanwhile, the gathering crowd was narrowing the circle, gripping us in a huge, unfriendly embrace. Someone was exclaiming loudly, someone was whispering convulsively, but nobody was moving to call an ambulance. And only when the atmosphere was strained to its limit and in many aspects beyond its limit, did the dying man "rescue" *us*. He moved his shoulders, as if freeing them from an unbearable load, helplessly stretched out his hands for the last time, stopped breathing and went limp. In the depressing silence that followed there was a minute when we could hear a seller of magazines fidgeting at the end of the tunnel. In other words, in the silence there was a decisive moment when the crowd parted, letting through the most respected, trusted and valued member of society. In such cases, a solid citizen coughs with significance once or twice, taking the lead, and then starts reciting pompously: "Life has its end, but death is limitless. We live for a short while and die for ever." God damn it, that guy is incredible; he definitely isn't worth his salt! He created the epic scene that was worthy of being put on a big stage by a prominent theatrical director... but somehow *nobody* stepped forward. Nobody recited. Instead, everyone stood still for some time, shaking their heads, and then the crowd broke up silently. Curiosity satisfied, everybody plunged into selfish indifference again. That was the logical end of the performance. The curtain!

So many striking events in one day, endless, free gifts, but my question remained unanswered. Had the supervisor's death contributed beneficially to our lives or made our fate worse? Is everyone's life more valuable than anything in the world or, on the contrary, totally worthless? You probably didn't think of anything, rejoicing as though the murder that had just occurred was your personal victory.

"For the first time in our life we've had the luck to win the game. Don't you think so?" you asked severely.

Hope, I know, cruelty always gives rise to cruelty, anger begets hatred, but I wonder if you could really wish upon him such a death?

"Let's say we wish only good for everybody," you elaborated your own thought. "Wouldn't we already be strangled, robbed, murdered by people like him?" and you nodded towards the armless man.

I perfectly understood what you were trying to say. If you think of people kindly it doesn't mean that people think of you the same way too. But, still, I couldn't agree with you. Call me impractical or stupid, but I want things to be different. Furthermore, we must make things different. Secondly, I consider it wrong and weird that we did not understand each other, although we saw and felt everything simultaneously. To hell with this motor adynamia.

"You're a fool," you blurted out. "You should be happy that someone else killed him. Otherwise you would have had to do the job yourself."

And, having touched your broken lip, you added indulgently:

"And by the way, where did that stinky snippet disappear to? Did he really run to get some vodka?"

Indeed, hardly had we merged into the crowd again than had our "pumpkin companion" immediately dived in from the opposite direction. I thought that he would never come back, but in a couple of days he appeared and, heartily begging our pardon, handed us a bottle.

"I could only procure this sort," he drawled in the tone of an apologetic child, baring his front teeth with a gap between them wide enough to insert a pencil, smiling in a conciliatory fashion.

"What's the freaking difference? Give me what you've got," you grumbled. "Why did you stick to us?"

His artless face instantly strained, and his fingers shuffled all over his body, so he had to clasp them to his chest.

"I will certainly explain," he said in a mournful voice. "I will tell you everything, exactly how it is. Please don't take offence; all my life, only a few moments have mattered."

He had been withholding this story for so long that once he found "grateful listeners" in our persons, he burst out, telling us more than we ever needed to know. His speech was filled with clichés from beginning to end, probably taken from newspapers randomly, forming an aura of a man of education and culture. He received quite a trivial nickname at school: Ickie, which irritated him terribly, but one can't be angry all the time. Soon, he got tired, then resigned himself and was finally convinced of the "truthfulness" of his nickname. With this regard, one person dear to me who preferred to die for his real name should be remembered. But Ickie was of quite a different breed, for he was ready to agree with any label in order to feel safe and unstressed. Only much later did we learn his real surname: either Poop or Poopie, which wasn't really good. On the contrary, "Ickie" suited him much better.

I wonder whether he was nicknamed thoughtlessly, as a result of a "harmless", childish prank, and only years later did he unknowingly start to fulfil his nickname! Did he turn a flight of somebody's ridiculous fancy into reality on purpose, trying to please everyone, or was he a grub and a sloven initially, being Ickie from the very beginning? I guess we'll never know what was behind that door.

When he turned thirteen, he went abroad with his parents, aerial artists, who had several performances a day. In the meantime, instead of training and gaining experience, he used to run away from the circus-troop and walk around the city. Well, as always happens in real life and rarely in fairy tales, once upon a time he accidentally wandered into a fair, and, driven by a mysterious inner instinct, sneaked into a circus-tent.

At first, the announcer appeared in the arena to make a speech about people's destinies – how many misfortunes and gross injustices we happen to encounter in life; but it is really not our fault, and we cannot do anything about it. He didn't want to persuade anyone to seek a reason for the surprising phenomenon that followed, but to accept it as "given", and try to laugh together *as a family*. At last, the lights were turned down low and a few moments later incredible creatures, like from a scary story, one after another, rolled out onto the arena riding unicycles. At first he thought it was a freakish effect of the light or a dodgy trick, but after a closer look, he understood. These were real people in front of his eyes... very ugly people, dwarfs with big heads, giants with small ones, athletes without arms, and people resembling animals. The public was ecstatic, giving them a standing ovation that suddenly developed into a deafening squall when the leading lady, a real beauty with two pairs of legs, appeared in the arena. "If you could have seen her dancing," Ickie admired, wringing his hands. "She flew over the rows of seats like a feather; her skirt delightfully fluttered in the air as she stretched her tattooed body, exposing two pairs of charming legs in white, silk stockings." She was so neat and airy that he was uncontrollably attracted to her, and before she could even finish her performance, he found himself clambering up on the rope and jumping between rafters, showing his adeptness of bodily control to the four-legged leading lady. The audience, who took his acrobatic attempts as part of the show, laughed approvingly and with words and gestures of curiosity encouraged him in bravery. But the problem of how to get down solved itself: he fell down as a disobedient baby bird falls down from the maternal nest. "I'm lucky I didn't crash to my death," Ickie concluded colorlessly, as if doubtful of his very own sanity. "I broke nearly every bone in my body that day, but wasn't successful in making friends with her."

From that day on, probably embracing us as his "twin souls", Ickie came to see us almost daily, as if it were a fixed rendezvous. Entirely confused and disordered, he had consistently held areas that were established and limited from the very first day. Apologizing every time, he gave us a bottle of vodka, then went to the opposite wall and watched us, now one, now the other, moving his pupils like pendulums. Eventually, despite his intolerable smell and deep-rooted untidiness, I started kind of liking him and gradually getting used to his presence like some people get used to an offensive nickname.

As soon as our working day was over, we hurried home, to our old abandoned house, passionately wishing to get drunk. It just so happened that we didn't have any glasses and had to drink straight from the bottle, taking turns. We had yesterday's sprats and processed cheese; allow me to put this directly: not the most appropriate combination, but at that moment it was just right and surprisingly delicious! First we began by drinking with disgust, but then, sip by sip, the detestable taste seemed to disappear.

"To your health," I said, sipping from the bottle.

"To our health!" you exclaimed emotionally. "Have you already noticed? You are drinking but I'm the one who's got the hiccups?"

"Look, I can't drink anymore," I begged after half an hour.

"Then give me the bottle," you commanded. "I'm gonna drink for both of us, and we'll be getting drunk together, like communicating vessels."

Unexpectedly, we found this thought very amusing and burst out laughing in unison. The evening turned out to be an unprecedented one. I perceived you not only as my sister, my other half I am attached to, but primarily as a friend and a drinking companion. I was talking incessantly, about hilarious things, I guess, which I can hardly remember now, and you were smiling contentedly to yourself without any sense to your expression of bliss. Then one of us started singing, and gradually our howl developed into drunken crying. Each of us plunged into her own, seemingly very deep, sorrow, although we had no obvious reason to cry. After finishing the bottle, we went to bed, but stumbled and fell half way. It made us laugh anew, after which we fell asleep right there on the floor.

That night I had a dream of us dancing together in the circus arena. There were only two spectators: the pug supervisor and the armless tsar. They shouted something special and tried to applaud, but couldn't. One of them had no arms and the other was dead. And while we were spinning around in the spotlights, I saw an unspeakable envy on their faces. The whole world made a low bow to us because we were beautiful and unique.

Tomorrow Was the Country

What do I remember about summer? The smell of hot, freshly-laid asphalt, lonely passersby exhausted with heat, dashing sparrows in puddles, and a new supervisor – haughty, practical, convinced of his importance. Beggars nicknamed him Compass Legs without deliberating, which suited him pretty well. With his very long legs, always astride, his hands behind his back, narrow, sloping shoulders and oblong head, he really resembled a huge compass. His first philosophical remark and the following typical question puzzled us all:

"One always leads another, as if the devil himself has tied a rope around the pair of you. How did you get used to it?"

He had a somber but lively expression on his face while speaking; a compassionate voice completed the whole look.

Well, actually we didn't get used to it; we were born that way. Leading each other is the norm for us.

"Neither of us decides which foot to step on, where to go, when to stop - it just comes without prior arrangement," I explained, choosing my words carefully.

"Only our brains work independently," you added scornfully.

Compass Legs put his legs apart, as thin as matches, even more widely apart, and bewilderment, natural in every unfamiliar situation, revealed itself on his lanky face. It was the way a three-armed person might appear surprised witnessing how someone can do everything perfectly well with just two arms.

"We are always inseparable. We walk together and we sleep together, and it is impossible for one of us to sit at a table while the other is lying on a bed," I tried to joke.

"Yes, I can't remember that happening," you quipped again. "Though I wish I could."

"And, of course, you pee together, don't you?" Quite contented with his sagacity, he waved his hands and laughed.

I just shrugged my shoulders: laughter is much better than disgust. And Compass Legs, having sussed a special spirit, started rattling off like a machine gun, shooting questions:

"How fast can you run? Have you ever ridden a bicycle? Have you ever shared one man? Do you feel your body as a whole?"

"And does he feel his pathetic legs separately from his body?" I had this question on the tip of my tongue but didn't dare to ask. We tried to answer him in detail with a certain amount of imagination and humor. And he was rejoicing and laughing like a little boy who has been gifted with an unusual toy for his birthday. "I can only hope that, while playing, he won't tear off our limbs to see what's inside," I thought in dismay. Anyway, he behaved quite friendly and welcomed us, but I still kept waiting for the catch. Here, underground, nobody believes in nice, kind-hearted people, same as above ground!

I still remember the day we dropped into a nearby store. It used to be a grocery store, but now it sold everything but groceries, and with the money we had earned by unlawful begging, we bought a little dream – a china statuette of a ballerina. We saw it for the first time in winter, and every time we passed by, we envied the fragile, dancing swan – her beautiful body frozen in a graceful pose, her expressive arms resembling the wings of a rising bird, and her nice-shaped legs.

True perfection! Ever after, the china doll lit up my spirit and captured my soul: yes, yes, it was not a usual figurine anymore but a symbol of unattainability. The very first thought when I took her in my hands was to take a proper swing and smash her on the tiled floor in order to eliminate the source of intolerable pain and destructive sentiments – the difference. *We are different.* But despite the initial impulse of self-preservation, I passionately pressed the ballerina to my chest, so tightly that not even a thousand malicious supervisors would have been able to tear it out of my hands, white from the strain. I imagined that the doll and I were one harmonious whole and that all my lameness flowed into her faultless, dancing body.

She is still spinning around, then breaking down, falling, coiling in agony, and transforms herself into clumsy, unfree, imperfect me. As for you, somehow you didn't even touch her!

Having set the ballerina down in front of other things, I felt so tired as if I hadn't slept all night long. The following day, spent in the tunnel, feeling restless and antsy, made it seem as if the desired purchase and my own identity were merged. I didn't like it. In the evening I felt even worse, and you had to drag both of us... into nowhere. We found out that our nest didn't exist anymore – the house was totally destroyed. Instead we saw heaps of bricks, twisted beams and a crane with a huge weight on a chain towering nearby in stately eminence. Our household for years suddenly collapsed, as always, aided by people.

"It's good that we spent our last bit of money on this damned doll," you said, breathing a sigh of relief. "Lose faster to find sooner."

We still had the main valuables we had always possessed: our faith and hope, plus a fairly shabby drawing by Lizzie and an old blanket on our shoulders. Everything else was unimportant; our past seemed flat, as if made of cardboard, like hastily nailed together background scenery. Isn't it odd how the kindest and purest things that are of paramount importance lose their former attractiveness over time and start looking superficial, ordinary, and even alien? Having played their role, all unimportant and unnecessary things eventually die off, remaining in the past forever, while futures, our own included, lie beyond old, demolished houses.

We spent the night at Ickie's place. His apartment was filled with such a viscous and sticky smell that, once we stepped over the threshold, we felt like all the filth was steadily sucking us into its putrescent bog. Caustic, sour stench hung everywhere like a dense veil. It appeared we could touch it and define its color; the bathtub became green and was covered with slime, as if it was sick with a cold; the floor had gotten soaked through and rotted, making parquet boards plaintively creak with "save our souls" requests; the lighting was dim and faint as if hope had extinguished there and then. And the owner matched his icky apartment quite well.

Rolling clumsily, he took us to one of three rooms, folded out a couch and prepared bed linen; and while he messed around making us a bed, sweat streamed down his dirty face, dripping on to a scuzzy sheet. Having finished, he tiredly sank into the only armchair in the room and gazed at us with half-closed eyes, smiling guiltily and quietly sniffing; a slice of apple peel stuck to his front teeth. Time seemed to forget itself in conflict with the problems of the human heart. Time snored.

"Would you like me to take photos of you?" Ickie broke the silence and started fiddling with his fingers as if playing an invisible flute. "I do this sometimes when I am in the right mood and have inspiration, for my friends only."

"What the heck do you want it for?" you flashed. "Don't you see us often enough?"

"It's just a keepsake box," he told us sheepishly. "I merely collect photos. Would you like to take a look?"

Not even waiting for our yes, Ickie reached under the couch and took out an old cake box lovingly tied up with a colored ribbon.

"Here you are, my precious. Come on, don't be shy, I'm gonna show you to everybody," he muttered, carefully handing it over to us. And while we untangled the ribbon with a vague presentiment of something raunchy and obscene, Ickie hopped, blushing and nearly bursting with delightful confusion.

The box contained a pile of photos; well, it took me some time to understand whom they depicted. From every picture, a lot of different women looked at us, and one feature, except for their absolute nakedness, was common to them all: each woman had a prominent defect. There were one-eyed women, women with burns, lame, one-armed, bald, scarred - a full range of abnormalities one could only imagine.

"Holy crap, you're sick!" you cried, totally offended.

"Quiet, I'm begging you, quiet," Ickie fidgeted anxiously, waving his hands. "I share the most intimate things, from the bottom of my heart, and you are swearing. Too bad you don't like them. That's what I thought, people are prejudiced. Why are you throwing them away? There's no need to hurt them."

I saw a glimpse of fear in his eyes and in his gesture, as he rushed to pick up the pictures you had scattered, not even trying to keep the miserable shreds of his human dignity.

"In that case, I'll leave you," he said as if insulted, but didn't move, patiently waiting for our reaction. But you didn't say a word; we had no place to go.

"Just don't take offence," he babbled finally, tying up the box with a ribbon. "Maybe, after all, you will change your mind because such *gifts* shouldn't be wasted. I'm trying for everyone's benefit. Believe it or not, I might pay you if you need. I want to help."

"You have already helped," I responded quick-wittedly, "really helped. Thank you."

After my "thankfulness" Ickie lit up.

"Anyway, I should go. I'll be near, behind the wall, just in case," he twittered confusedly and poured out of the room, embracing his box.

The next morning Ickie flitted around us like a may bug, mumbling delightfully: "What a pleasure, what happiness!" And only after we had closed the bathroom door in his face – he must have peeped in at the keyhole – did we manage to obtain a degree of privacy which enabled us to wash ourselves and our clothes.

The same morning we asked Compass Legs to find housing for us. Usually talkative, this time he only hemmed gloomily and, having taken away our daily "yield", silently made his way.

We had to spend several more days at Ickie's. Challenges that we cannot even imagine! We who weren't used to convenience and comfort, we who had lived a significant part of our lives in the scrap heap, found it intolerable torment to stay at his place. Driven by an impulse of socially acceptable behavior, I offered to clean up his apartment, but didn't have much success in that endeavor. Absent-mindedly, shifting from one foot to the other, Ickie pretended that he didn't hear me, and hid in another room immediately after. A kettle whistled on the stove, indicating that it was time to have tea and go to work. But at the last minute, Ickie crept out of his shelter and called to us:

"Please, just don't take offence. I want everything to stay the same, the way it was when my mom was alive. I loved her so much, one and only."

You mysteriously looked around and stared at him closely: "I wonder if she felt the same way."

He got embarrassed and confused, and started waving his hands in a ridiculous fashion in front of his own nose as if fanning away a cloud of mosquitoes. Freckled, lop-eared, with a puppy look in his eyes and a timid smile, he looked like an old, blowsy, forlorn child. It seemed he had not only broken his arms and legs when he fell from the flying trapeze, but had also damaged some secret mechanism of ageing. Not waiting for an answer, we quietly passed through the door, leaving him alone with his crusted thoughts and infinitely dirty and unwelcome environment.

In a couple of days, the supervisor offered us housing in a desolate attic, and before we had time to answer, barked:

"Do push-ups! I want to see it," and added severely: "Come on, on the count of one-two."

Bewildered, I was at a loss what to do next and felt your hand dipping into a pocket in search of a screwdriver. Or could it be lipstick?

"All right, I'm kidding." The supervisor suddenly became cheerful. "I could force you, I have no desire. Let's skip it. You will work off your housing in a regular way. You should be happy that I am kind-hearted."

And we were happy that he helped us, that he didn't beat us, that he didn't force us to do push-ups or whatever, that he simply didn't drive us away. There will always be someone to replace us. No one's irreplaceable. That summer the number of beggars increased so strikingly that it seemed the whole country was begging with outstretched hands.

Yeah, we were really lucky. After the poverty, the dirt and the cold, the new housing we were provided with struck us as warm and cozy: scantily lit premises with high sloping ceilings of wooden beams smeared with pigeon dung here and there, brick walls with small windows under roofs that seemed about to fall, a heap of "accurately" laid plywood on a concrete floor and a weak, barely perceptible, unpleasant smell. A more thorough examination revealed the presence of small piles of faeces spread out carefully and evenly – not in just one corner, but literally everywhere – along the entire perimeter. We even had an urge to contribute ourselves. However, after many hours of cleaning, the attic began shining like a baby's butt and turned into a model to follow, a dream, an unrealizable wish; in a word, a place for normal life.

Ickie took the news about our new dwelling surprisingly calmly. Only after several minutes of contemplating dark streaks on the ceiling and heaving deep sighs did his true thoughts and emotions express themselves in words.

"These are times when everything is valued," he said with his eyelids drooping: "odd galoshes, empty bottles and even yesterday's newspapers, but pure, sincere feelings are depreciated and thrown out like household garbage, like something shameful and useless."

"Come on, stop whining," you blurted out. "We saw your inclinations, and thank you very much for that."

You sounded ironic, but Ickie, apparently, didn't notice it. Taking it literally, he straightened and answered rapidly:

"I am so glad, so glad, with all my heart. I mean it. My inmost secrets and everything, just everything, including my humble dwelling, is from now on at your disposal."

And his shoulders started jittering with wheedling laughter, or was he sneezing, not laughing? With Ickie, I couldn't shake off a strange feeling that all this had already happened to us many times before, and not long ago. He reminded me of a clock hand, always passing through the same events in strict accordance with a universal schedule. When he was done jittering, he went to the opposite wall. Picking a dirty spot on his vest, he stared at us; his eyes were shining with lust for the flesh and with unspeakable triumph.

So what I did actually was, I studied the certain issue from all sides and found something quite surprising. Some people look at us with disgust because we are unnatural, while others, on the contrary, admire us because we are unnatural, an admiration that is no less deformed than we ourselves are! "Poor Ickie, his life is so sad and monotonous," I thought, watching him go. "He is trapped in debilitating gloom and fatuity and there is no way to save him." But only now do I understand that he was actually happy, in his own way. It is not important that his life became so fouled up, extremely boring and antisocial. Above all, he felt warm and cozy in his own world even if it was not obvious, and everything else didn't matter. He never judged anyone and didn't have much interest in ordinary people. He thought their lives were as pathetic and ruined as they believed his life was. But once a three-legged or one-armed person appeared, the look in his eyes changed dramatically, and life quite unexpectedly acquired fresh colors and sense. Ickie didn't quit the dream of dedicating his life to the circus, but the whole world around him turned into a circus. And we *validated* it all, happening by chance to participate in some of his *improvised* performances, too!

I have only fragmentary memories of our former life. Everyday routine accelerates time, letting it flow away and be lost. However, I remember, one winter we were standing in the tunnel, and a passerby, looking like an ordinary guy who came out of the crowd, thrust a fifty ruble banknote into my hand. By the evening we already had four fifty ruble bills. Furthermore, in the daylight people came to us and offered to exchange paper money for small change, giving us extra payment. We were literally shining with happiness, as we had an opportunity to earn more – five, ten, or sometimes twenty times as much as usual; and it didn't even come to our minds that there was a reason for such generosity[21]. Well, when the supervisor came, he just got furious and tore all the large denomination bills into shreds, muttering:

"Dumbasses, another time I'll tear you up."

Taking away all our collected small change and pushing away one of the cripples, he poured out of the tunnel. Same as his deceased predecessor, the pug, Compass Legs couldn't understand the basics: there's nothing great in humiliating those who are on the receiving end. "What can I say," after being knocked down, the cripple grumbled dimly, expressing everyone's opinion: "Foolish is as foolish does."

By a twist of fate, we turned out to be in a special environment, the special environment where things can be seen most clearly. The tunnel was our auditorium, with daily classes in psychology and philosophy. We secretly watched people reckless, sly, rejecting all the best created by previous generations in pursuit of a better life: tearing former pictures, throwing out old books, changing erstwhile slogans – swearing

---

21   Monetary reform of 1991 in the USSR - exchange of large denomination banknotes carried out in the USSR in January-April, 1991. Exchange of the withdrawn notes was followed by essential restrictions:

• Short deadlines of exchange - three days from January 23 to January 25 (Wednesday to Friday).

• No more than 1000 rubles per one person; the possibility to exchange the bills beyond that limit was considered by special commissions until the end of March, 1991.

The reform resulted in a loss of trust of the population in the government's actions.

off anything valuable in the country's history. Thoughts of survival became rooted in people's minds so deeply and tenaciously that all principles of conscience were discarded as useless, and only "saving" alcohol could quench the thirst for oblivion and idleness. Those times we didn't drink very often and exchanged vodka, which had became a principal means of payment, for food or services. The prices rose daily[22], but life just kept getting worse the more alms we received. Probably, misfortune unites people. In those moments they were particularly capable of compassion for other people's grief. Losses, disappointments and imperfections that had filled the country made passersby feel much more similar to each other than ever before.

And then that old acquaintance of ours, the blind gipsy, appeared. I felt severely sick that day; maybe that's why I clearly remembered her widely open, motionless eyes looking away but seeming to see through. Having rummaged in the depths of her pocket, she took out an old coin which was no longer in circulation, and threw it on the ground in front of us.

"Thank you," I couldn't help saying.

"Keep your thank you notes for later. Today I'm going to tell Compass Legs," she perfectly knew his moniker, "to shift you to another spot."

"What's the sense?" We were surprised simultaneously.

---

22   This refers to price liberalization or price deregulation - element of the economic policy of the Russian government in the early 1990s involving weakening of government control over pricing.
Price liberalization led to increases in prices considerably exceeding the growth of money supply, resulting in its real compression. Thus, the GDP deflation index and the consumer price index increased approximately 2400-fold from 1992 to 1997, and M2 monetary aggregate increased approximately 280-fold for the same period.

"Always and everywhere there is a sense," she responded patiently. "Today I'm helping you, tomorrow you're helping somebody, and then someone will help *me*. And another thing, if someone touches you with a shadow of his little finger, just tell me."

"But how do we find you?" you wondered.

"I will find *you*," and this muddy-eyed fish smiled with her gold teeth and yelled so loud that she could be heard all over the tunnel. "Well, precious ones, see you here or there. Keep in touch."

A new spot again, and how many of them are going to appear throughout our lifetime? No one knows.

The next day Compass Legs rapidly explained our new "working" conditions to us. We gave him all our money, collected for the day in exchange for free food and accommodation. Indeed, why take away a part if you can take away the whole!? Supervisors know their business: a person – in our case, two persons – who has no choice can be easily twisted around your little finger.

"I can't do this anymore," I decided to share my thoughts with you.

You turned away, trying to hide your face, and at that very moment I saw your reflection in the kiosk window – helpless, crocked and embittered.

"We can't quit, you must understand, we have nowhere to go," you said, choosing the words with difficulty. "However, Ickie's maternal dwelling or better yet a madhouse would accept us with open arms."

Suddenly and without any warning, your eyes flashed with malicious fire:

"Here we're uncommonly but not improperly taken for a very young woman, I mean, two women. And in the mental home, what is expected of us? Now I say that walking from corner to corner, pills, dirty bedpans and special treatment which makes us really and permanently madwomen; and nobody's even going to listen to you – you are a loony, you are of no use for anything. Running away is not an option because there is no place to escape. We have to survive with a limited number of options, that's the only thing we should think about. Society determined with great precision that we belong to the rubbish dump; we have to take it and be grateful for it. Here, we are at least given a chance for some kind of existence."

You became silent for a while, moving your finger on a glass, and then continued:

"Our underground world is not so bad. It is governed by certain rules, which may be cruel, but they work perfectly fine for me. Up above, there are no rules at all, especially for the needy like us; just sadness, depression and gloom."

A burdensome feeling of unease and sickness that is hard to put into words was gradually fading away until it disappeared completely. From that moment on, I tried not to bring up the issue of escape anymore because I was sincerely afraid: what if you suggest the old proven way of solving problems: jumping out of a window?

It is generally accepted that if you have ugly looks, you must be beautiful inside. That's what classic books say. Lies! Only here, in our place, you understand how far the authors are from reality. The truth is, the more hardships a person is going through, the more exasperated he or she becomes. A new tunnel reminded me of a tumultuous river with a flock of beggars nestling ashore; they met us "at the door" with such undisguised hatred that we even had to close our eyes tight. There was nothing but the malice we were already used to; nothing but new concerns and privations which we were somehow meant to get through.

A Day Sober Is a Day Wasted

Ickie found us three days later. That was how long it took him to search through half of the walking tunnels under the city. We left our spot to fulfill a physical need while he agreed to substitute us in our begging business.

"Help, please, good people. Don't just walk on by, make a donation," Ickie squealed, expressing all the grievances of the world and puffing out his shiny, sweaty cheeks. When we returned, he had already raised a fairly decent amount of cash. The only thing I could say about that was: whoever is a real nothing is capable of many things.

Making our way back to our spot in the half-dark, we nearly ran into a "newcomer". It took me some time to actually recognize her, because the woman standing in front of us was a totally different person. Fear and desperation had bent her back completely, against her will, as if somebody dispatched Sprinter – yes, yes, that was really her – to another planet and replaced her with a pathetic, miserable woman looking exactly like her mom, whom we have never seen. In addition, now she was called Teeter-Totter, probably because of her rolling gait. The reunion reminded her of foster-home days which she wanted to forget. Recognizing us immediately, although there was a crowd of people around, she became completely abashed, shrank into herself, and grew dim, contorted with a mixture of horror and shame. We continued looking at each other for some time, not knowing what to say. A painful and unwanted meeting with the past. I couldn't understand how she had ended up here. Later, Compass Legs gave us a brief summary of her life, actually not even a summary, just a few words. "She got kicked out of technical school, and then banished from her roost; now she lives with some drunkard; besides, she's lazy and slow, not eager to work." And that was it! No names, no dates, no fate. And, what's most important: she is just an ordinary beggar, just like all of us. This thought was both new and honey-sweet to my heart, which filled with malicious joy. I hate to admit it, but boy was I pleased! Why?

While I was pondering whether I should bend my knees in submission or spit at her as a greeting, Ickie stealthily slid behind us and diffused the situation. He told us a strange story of how he had been surprisingly hurt in the best of his feelings when a terminally ill woman he had fallen in love with had started recovering *all of a sudden*, with such a touching expression and so comically waving his hands that involuntarily he made everybody laugh. For the first time in our life I saw Sprinter laughing.

"You're such an attractive woman, a perfect model to be drawn," Ickie cackled spiritedly. "But I can only offer you a photo of yourself. It's not a painting, of course, but it's still a keepsake weapon which I plan on using for the delight of your soul."

After our refusal he still had some idea of how he might replenish his collection with new images.

Having thought for a moment, Sprinter, or Teeter-Totter, screwed her face into a smile and replied:

"Well, I don't mind delighting my soul. This I am willing to do."

As a goodbye, Ickie at first kissed her on the cheek, and then shook her hand twice, probably just to clinch the deal, to seal the bargain. Then he stood for a while, shyly and ingratiatingly looking her in the face and, after making an apology, left – and later...

What happened later? One evening, after a working day, Ickie invited us to a backstreet boozer, as dirty as his apartment. He was a little bit jittery, staring at us nervously, hesitating and not knowing where to start as if a girl he had been dating for a long time took her friend with her when he decided to confess his feelings. After five minutes of waiting you couldn't stand it anymore:

"So, what happened? Spit it out!"

"I'm getting married," Ickie blurted out, and you shuddered with surprise.

He was so desperate to look impassive, as if the talk was about an old friend, but his hands showed his condition, fidgeting, shivering, and from time to time letting out a mute "shout".

"You're a lying jerk! Whoever's gonna take an interest in you?" you spat out with eyes flashing with hatred.

He didn't answer, just clasped his hands around him tightly, trying to join them behind his back, and started coughing discontentedly.

"If she was humpbacked or didn't have a foot or an eye, then you shouldn't hesitate to marry her. But she is, to my unspeakable horror, merely lame. What's so special about limping? Not your style, Ickie!" you said very rudely.

I didn't realize at that moment you were talking about an old acquaintance of ours. From the first day, she did her best to try and please Ickie. She shook the dust out of his house and cleaned the dirt off his clothes, cared and helped him, even cured his ailments. Yeah, Sprinter chose a truly non-losing strategy, searching for survival outside the tunnel, not inside.

"Don't be offended, but it's the first time someone needs me after my mom," he said, sobbing silly with happiness. "I know we're meant for each other."

Was that love or just abstemiousness, driven to an extremity?

It was totally unexpected. At first I didn't like him at all, but after a while I got used to Ickie and didn't want to lose him. He's been there for us all this time, having actually become the third twin in our pack. Besides that, along with him, the vodka would also disappear. Before leaving, Ickie delivered so many needless, faceless clichés that if anything noteworthy was ever glimpsed there, it would remain unnoticed.

"I'll come tomorrow," he assured us, and his face contorted with a forced smile.

But, of course, he didn't come the next day, or any day after that. He didn't come in a week, in a month. It didn't matter whether he avoided us by a whim of circumstance or willfully forgot about our existence; whatever happened, we were left alone again. However, before going away, Ickie seemed to have deliberately endowed us with bitter thoughts on love and all of its little white lies – his last gift implicating the promises of illusive happiness and its feasibility.

At some point I started noticing that you were no longer alone in the woods – Compass Legs showed a keen interest in you. From time to time he treated you with a cigarette, pinched you or made a corny joke.

"What a soothing voice he has!" you exclaimed dreamily as we went outside. "I wish I was alone... Anyway, Compass Legs is not Ickie," you smiled sadly. "It's a pity, but he won't be bringing us vodka."

Afterwards, I often thought about your words. For the first time in our life I was a heavy burden for you, or was it just the first time you let it out? I saw Compass Legs in a totally different light: a wry smirk instead of a smile, piggy eyes resembling buttons; raunchy, stupid, speaking awkwardly and always irrelevantly. But hardly had I started "unmasking" him when you pounced upon me with insults or covered your ears, shaking your head. How seldom can even the closest people understand each other.

"Am I worthy of being loved?" you asked, suddenly anxious, alluding to Compass Legs.

Deprived of everything that constitutes a woman and in general a human essence – family, motherhood, men's attention, interesting and rewarding work – you were compelled to stand in the stinking tunnel for days, extorting the sympathy of passers-by, mixed with disgust. No wonder that yearning for love had arisen in your mind as a manifestation of natural human impulses and desires. Infinitely humiliated, you asserted your dignity through love.

Did I become your enemy then by telling you the truth? The question that must not be answered, but I found the answer! The very moment you asked this question my heart started thumping, poisoned with jealousy, and my stubborn silence spoke more than any words.

"Why am I asking you? What can you possibly know about how I feel?" You grew furious, and, unfortunately, you were right. I didn't know anything then and I don't know anything now! There is no museum which stores a standard of true love against which to compare your own perceptions.

"Just think about what he could give us: protection, a good job, better housing and, perhaps, even a TV," you were cackling as silly as Ickie used to some time ago.

I believed those reasonable arguments were there to hide your true feelings. You got attracted to him strongly, right away – for some physical reason, *inconceivable to me*, - but were afraid to admit it. Meanwhile, having yielded to your request, Compass Legs started bringing vodka to you. Maybe he really liked you? Who knows! I saw in his acts no more than encouragement for his best "workers" in the tunnel. We had earned him so much money with our begging, and we all got a poor thank-you – vodka – but you took it as a declaration of care and love. In fact, everything started with it.

But first, something else happened.

Probably, sooner or later, every person finds himself to be disposable. He appeared before us in short, badly-faded trousers with an open zipper, with lean hands and huge bags under his eyes, all tousled like a sparrow after bathing in a puddle. He smelled of medication and something acrid, perhaps garlic or onions. His glasses had only one temple, shoes were put on bare feet, without socks, and the whole image was completed with a gloomy face and a wan smile baring mostly empty gums on top and an uneven number of metal teeth on the bottom. He approached us, dragging his body and creaking like an old cart. Leaning against a wall, we stiffened in expectation, wondering who he was and not knowing what he wanted. For some time he hesitated, choosing which one of us to look at and who to address. And when he, after much hesitation, started talking, all the futility of life was expressed in his voice. He used to work as a major chief engineer, helping to design parts for future carrier rockets. In due time, he had retired and spent the last of his savings that had remained after monetary reforms on some government securities promising enormous profit, but afterwards he went broke and lost everything. Although his entire look emitted absolute infirmity and hopelessness, he was telling us about his failures in such a tone as if they were his main virtues. "Idiot," I thought, "if you prefer being proud of your suffering – well, please, go to church! But why are you sticking strangers with it?"

"Everything is lost and ruined, but I am still alive, being older than Byron and Lermontov put together," he finished joyfully and a little haughtily.

"Do you at least have a wife?" I asked, out of curiosity. "Byron did."

Instead of answering, he grew sad instantly and looked away, silently moving his lips.

"Any children?"

Very slowly, almost imperceptibly, a small, aged and decrepit person who used to be great and important nodded his bowed head. When he started talking again, his voice sounded different. It appeared that more than twenty years ago his wife had given birth to boys, conjoined twins, exactly like us! At the time of delivery he was away on business and kept putting off meeting his babies on the pretext of being busy. And when he did return, when everything was over, realizing his cowardice, his wife took the children away to an undisclosed location, but that was just the beginning – for after a few months she wrote to him about their early deaths, the small revenge of a resentful woman.

"Am I a coward?" he questioned, clamping his head between his hands. "I used to think the contrary. I had been working my ass off, sometimes hadn't been leaving my studio for months, fearlessly looked slanderers and tale-bearers in the face. I wasn't afraid of anything, but seeing two conjoined..." he faltered, at a loss for words, "two poor babies was beyond my power. Soon we got divorced, and for many years I haven't heard from her. Then one day, totally unexpected, as it usually occurs only in the movies but never in reality, I ran into her in the street of just another town where she was on a behind-the-scenes tour. Can you imagine the odds of that happening?" He raised his hands, addressing the muddy stains on the ceiling. "One in a million, no, actually, one in a billion. Either way, this encounter changed my life. My wife confessed that she had lied to me. In fact, the children were alive and under the care of the government. Right after childbirth she signed documents to transfer them to the institute of pediatrics. I begged and asked her for any further information, but she refused to provide me with any more details. I filed requests to state bodies, tried to search for any documents in the maternity home, but all I found was an old midwife who told me, for a small remuneration, that they were sent to a Scientific Research Institution and she had no idea to which one. My children just vanished into thin air," he grieved bitterly. "Since then I've been looking for them, unable to find them, but nevertheless have kept searching, now rather out of cowardice than for any other reason. I seem to carry on living only out of cowardice. Charity, alas, was so right."

His story was growing like a snowball, releasing more and more details which little by little came together. His former wife, a leading actress plus the number of maternity homes which we had learnt from our mother plus the year of birth, the same as ours, and so on and so forth. Only one thing was confusing: his conviction that he had sons. But could it be possible that everything else, even our mother's name, was a total match? As he said, the odds are one in a billion, no, one in a billion billion! And the aerospace engineer should have realized it like no one else, but still he couldn't or didn't want to see that we were his children. For us, the truth was much more obvious: this pathetic, skinny, silly, smiling man was *our father*.

Sometimes it seems to me that even chance events are rather predetermined. Our father had been looking for us all his life – he couldn't stop searching, tormented by his conscience – and, of course, he found us or, to be precise, stumbled upon us by chance like a moribund person stumbles upon a gem that he is no longer in need of. True, it was too late to change anything – his age was not good for major undertakings – and his dreams had not come to pass, mired in a swamp of nightmares. But nevertheless his fate winked at life in parting. Finally, in one last effort he had come across us to make sure once again that we were too great a challenge for him, too tough a nut to crack!

He died long ago, way before his time, on the same day we were born.

He didn't ask any questions, afraid to speak out unwittingly the major one: Are we those he has been looking for? Refusing to trust his own eyes, disregarding the evidence, he hid in his turtle shell in order not to reopen old wounds, in order to keep his mind sound. But did we have the right to blame him? Is there at least one person on earth who isn't afraid to face the truth and is capable of diving into its very heart, accepting it wholly? Are there people who don't lie at least to themselves?

We only saw him three times in our whole life. And every time, having caught sight of us, he rubbed his eyes as if chasing away a bad dream, and only after making sure we were real, did he approach reluctantly, keeping silent and dismally picking the floor tiles with his foot. At that moment, he felt no interest in absolutely anything he did, having lost his fire, his grip, his sense. And every time I saw him I wanted to cry, stamp my feet, run up to him and confess everything. But what is the point of doing something that is not correct? Our appearance undoubtedly hurt our family. We've been through it with our mother, and now our father's time has come. Should we push our luck for a second time? Actually, it was high time to bring an end to a wearisome connection with the past and turn into ordinary observers of another human tragedy. Pretending that *we are not them*, we withdrew from his life. Of course, we felt sorry for the father, but it was more compassion than love.

Very strong, obnoxious feelings come into our lives through sudden insight. You might unexpectedly feel something splitting off from your heart and wandering all over your body, like a tiny stone in a boot. There's nothing you can do about it: neither get used to it nor shake it out. I clearly saw us from the outside, like in a picture. We are not really human beings. We are a road-side sign warning people to stop and thank their lucky stars that such a fate as ours didn't befall them, and only then keep going their way. All right, but who is going to be a benchmark for us? What road sign is going to guide our voyage? It is so good that you're still asleep, and I can speak out and put into words every single thing on my mind.

I often think that, deep within, people agree to humiliation which steers them back on to the right path, but self-humiliation is more effective and sweeter. It just so happens that we represent the brightest example of it. With our appearance, we endlessly abase ourselves, thereby exalting people around us. Like snakes, we whisper in people's ears with forked tongues: "Look at us, worse things happen. Look at us." I think getting used to hard luck makes us even greater losers. A streak of troubles and mischiefs is infinite because it ruins our desire, will and aspiration to do something bigger and better. All that is left for us is boredom, a lack of faith and hopefulness.

Having realized that our shared illness is ourselves and not a mysterious force above us, I came across an even more amazing and odd thing that was actually forever present, forever obvious. Of the many great ways that exist to get cured of oneself, the most effective is to obliterate one's mind; and there is no greater help than alcohol. I even had my own idiotic theory: we get drunk to unlock our hidden secrets to the world, and every bad thing in life comes to a natural end eventually. However, this idea isn't a new one. But once we sober up, reality suddenly acquires its former outlines, forcing us to muffle up in a blanket again to resemble normal people, at least a little.

Vodka is a repulsive substance. The only good thing about it is the final feeling of booziness but, speaking frankly, even that can't and shouldn't be enjoyable! Anyway, we were drinking, dishonestly deceived and alienated from ourselves, imprisoned in a bottle like fairy tale djinns. The former synchrony of our acts completely disappeared. Sometimes simple movements, such as walking, getting up or sitting down took a great deal of time and effort as if we had to make summersaults or perform fanciful tricks. Having lost a sense of reality, we never hurried anywhere. We didn't know how long our intoxicated oblivion would last.

I remember one night I was woken up by an urgent physical need and tried to rattle you up, but in vain; so I had nothing left to do but relieve myself while lying on the floor. It felt wet and immensely loathsome all night long. Once again, we descended into hell but lived even worse than sinners.

Compass Legs knew about our drinking habit, but didn't see any tragedy in it. Most likely, we collected more alms *in that condition*, but I don't remember for sure. And one day, perhaps being overwhelmed with "gratitude" for our work, he invited us for a drink with his friends at a lousy boozer. You were certainly on cloud nine that day. All day long you hummed something that ended with "I wish I was alone" in a low tone, jigging up and down in excitement, and what angered me the most was your total lack of remorse. Again, I saw what you really were and greatly disliked it. It just so happened that you were the reason for so much more pain and suffering than people deserve, taken out on me, hurt by misfortune.

And yet I still loved you. Former Hope, strong, stout hearted, self-giving, capable of honorable actions, and present Hope, pathetic, embittered and rude. I loved "both" of you so much that I could have easily died for you if only I'd had the chance.

You kept silent. Why am I actually recounting all this? Whether it is a final attempt to talk my fears away, to muffle my cries of pain! Only the devil knows. In this smelly, rotten-through world I still crave to love without being loved back; it is the best antidote for pain and indifference. Love is what heals all wounds, not vodka. I believe – in love.

"Tell me, Faith, am I beautiful?" you asked, slowing down in front of an already closed store window. "Tell me the truth."

And suddenly something childish and naive appeared through your veil of ignorance and rudeness. So, this is where your intimate, purely woman's dream to be an object of admiration and desire has been hiding! With bated breath, I lovingly peered at the reflection in the window where a thin, small girl with long hair, an exact replica of myself, was snuggling to me. Suddenly my eyes got wet... because so many times I have looked at you and never realized how attractive you are. I was surprised that nobody could say it. Maybe people just can't stand beautiful freaks – or we might be beautiful only for each other.

"Sometimes you look at me so weirdly as if you're much older," giving a sigh, you commented on my thoughtful expression. "So, am I beautiful?"

Instead of answering, I rummaged in our pockets and took our mom's lipstick, then colored your lips and smoothed down your hair. Fastidiously examining your face from all sides, you applied one more layer of lipstick, just to make sure, and dropped carelessly:

"I think we should make you up too."

"No need to. Today I'm staying at home. You will go by yourself."

As you are well aware, we have been doing everything together for our entire life. Of course, I was extremely tired of it. And so many nights I just dreamt of staying alone with myself for a while but the worst thing you could do at that moment was to support me in this desire.

Having decided to drink myself insensible, I suggested finishing the bottle standing in the attic. My head instantly started buzzing and throbbing, and all of a sudden I became deadly sleepy, as if we were taking sleeping pills instead of vodka. I can only remember brief snippets of what happened next. Somehow I found us in a boozer sitting opposite Compass Legs and strenuously pretending that whatever was going on had no relevance to me. However, I was drinking beer along with everybody, and when I tried to get up – obviously, to go to the bathroom – the chair nearly seized you, holding me back. I was heavy, dizzy, and reality looked hostile. Objects were losing their usual shape, blurring and vanishing. I felt like I was going mad, slowly sinking into a deep abyss, until I fell into a dead faint, and darkness surrounded us, or just me.

People who have undergone a leg or an arm-amputation are said to feel their limbs as if they remained in place, but I am wondering whether they feel them just a moment before they lose them forever. As for me, I felt neither my arms, nor my legs, nor your bodily presence. Instead, I had a dream of being a little girl again, and you were holding me in your arms. You gave me a bright, good-natured smile, stroked my hair, touched my neck and then started strangling me, still smiling. Caught up in a frenzy of horror, I felt myself dying, suffocating in my sleep, then I started groaning and tossing and finally woke up.

My pulse was throbbing in my temples, my hands were trembling, but two bitter hearts were still beating in agreement. Turning to the right, I felt – sometimes it's more than seeing – you strangling yourself with a piece of old wire. By some miracle I twisted and slapped you in the face several times, not even realizing that all this time I was shrieking. You almost did it but ended up just gasping convulsively.

"Whyyyy?" I croaked. "Stop doing it! Drop it!"

I tried to kiss you on your forehead, cheeks, hair – everywhere I could reach, comforting you as a mother comforts her child, but the child didn't listen to me and wanted to die.

"Leave me alone. I hate you, I hate myself, I hate everyone," you whined plaintively and burst out crying; however, it resembled more of a blizzard's yearning howl than crying. I can't tell how long it lasted: five or ten minutes, one hour or a whole eternity.

"And what if you are going the *right* way?" I seemed to stop breathing, struck by that sudden thought. "Both of us are so tired of resisting, struggling, surviving and failing that there is no strength left to conquer the whole damn world. I give up too."

"First, kill me, then yourself. I'm not going to stop you. On the contrary, I will help," I said, putting my arms under my back and closing my eyes.

It is worth noting that killing yourself and killing someone else are not the same thing. For the former, you should lose faith; for the latter, you should never have any… Faith.

"Faith," you called to me, sobbing quietly, "tell me, why? We are not such bad people. I've seen worse than us. Especially this one… with skinny legs," you said hopelessly and lit a lantern.

"What happened?" I cried, squinting against the light. "Who are you talking about?"

"About Compass Legs, of course. Who could do much more evil?" you muttered dejectedly. "Don't you remember anything?"

I shook my head. I seemed to remember nothing.

"He started making moves on me and then, after pushing me, he stopped and said: "Oh, my gosh, I must be completely drunk if I tried to make you mine." You reminded me of the whole story and began to cry again. Through your tears you told me that it was you who started kissing him, not knowing how else to express your feelings for a man. For a moment I saw us with his eyes and felt nausea, shuddering with disgust. There is no more repulsive thing than a physiologically ugly person. Of course, in our own eyes we are just like everyone else, only more so – approximately twice as much; but how can we see through our own eyes anybody, let alone everybody else? For eyes are not lightbulbs, after all.

"Anyway, we're going to be dead," you whispered almost malevolently. "I tried to strangle him. Sorry."

"It's OK. Where there's life there's hope," I suddenly said with unexpected determination. "If we are still alive today, I don't see why we should die tomorrow."

And I was right. The next day Compass Legs gazed at us so intently that I felt uneasy. Nevertheless, without saying a word, he dispassionately gathered all our income, having checked our pockets for form's sake and went away. And I sincerely believed the same as you, that he didn't remember anything at all.

* * *

I am still trying to understand when or where our paths diverged. How did it happen and why? Failing to do away with yourself at one stroke, you took another approach – slow suicide. You drank a great deal of vodka that evening, hiding behind an upturned collar, turning away and not wishing to listen. Witnessing your guzzling, I felt an obnoxious dizziness and started shivering with rage because now you were becoming a person I hated. True, at that moment I wanted to knock you to the ground and kick you with my feet. You fell asleep sitting on the floor, and I had to drag our bodies; occasionally you helped me with your feet. Nine yards to the bed took me half an hour. As a result I couldn't bend my aching back, my arms disobeyed; besides, I got woozy from alcohol too, along with you, and had a delirious feeling that another, absolutely unknown and uninvited person came and lay down next to me instead of you. I wonder if one of us were to go insane, what would happen to the other. The same thing, I hope.

For a long time I couldn't sleep. In despair, I drank up the remains of the vodka. On my way to long-awaited and desired unconsciousness, I continued to think intensely about everything important and necessary, until the world fell into emptiness where universal questions were removed.

Since then, you have called vodka your best and only friend, saving your life from tough and tougher ordeals. I dare say you are partly right. Alcohol really helps us close our eyes in the face of danger, whether imaginary or real, and enables us to escape the truth as one old woman taught us once.

Little by little, we turned into two dogs hating each other and sitting on one short leash – our liver ached permanently. Feeling sick was now a normal condition. Nausea came up even more often than ever before. Our heads were splitting, bitter tastes in our mouths and painful hangovers which pursued us constantly. Many people believe that hope supports faith, but in our case, paradoxically enough, Hope was hindering Faith. It's funny. Maybe people really do have it all wrong with our names?

I'm talking on and on; it seems I really can get to the bottom of it all, to the truth. But you should understand I *need* to speak while you're asleep; this makes more sense to me than any ordinary conversation, and I can see clearly now that it wasn't love and patience but revenge and bitter hatred that helped us get to know each other much better.

I was aware that you hated me desperately, tied to me for the rest of our lives, and there was no way to change it. Retiring into your shell, you no longer lived our shared life, but a very quiet life of your own; in other words, you rejected me like a body rejects its own disobedient hand. It made me feel insupportable pain, depriving me of understanding what the next step or move was. Instead of doing something worthwhile, I chose to do nothing at all: neither move, nor speak, nor even breathe, pretending that I didn't exist. I stayed motionless, waiting for movement. Perhaps, I should have acted in a different way, should have anticipated your moods, softened your rages, tried to know your thoughts and to do whatever you desired. But pain, born out of hurt pride, was stinging me and I could only focus on myself and neglect others. Every day we became more aggressive and selfish, as if after leaving our mother you had caught her self-destructiveness and then infected me with it. Having turned into enemies, we hated each other more and more with each passing day. You scowled at me with hateful eyes and when you started drinking you couldn't stop. You did it not for the sake of getting drunk but in order to plague me. Thus, little by little, our connection faded away, until the only thing we had in common and the only thing left partially unbroken was our liver.

In those days I almost gave up, not expecting anything would change, that only a miracle could save us and put us back together.

Thank you, Yura, the space is ours!

All night long you were pushing and tossing, croaking and groaning, keeping me awake. I squeezed your hands tightly – they were hot and very dry – and studied the tension that you felt. As soon as we got out of bed, you threw up on the floor something that looked like rotten gruel.

"I got sick again," you sighed heavily and shook your head. "It's always the same: catching a cold, nursing a cold, then catching and nursing, over and over again."

"My bones ache," I confessed wearily. "Maybe we should not go to work today?"

"Would you like to spend all day in this smelly attic?" you responded angrily. "No way; you may stay if you want, but I'm going outside."

It became clear finally and irrevocably. You are something that destroys me, and there is no natural way to get rid of your existence.

In the frosty air, we felt a little better, and our spirits brightened. But in the tunnel you threw up again, though we hadn't eaten anything since yesterday morning. You were shivering all over; I knew my condition was lousy too; I had fever and cold chills. Out of the corner of my eye I saw your head droop very slowly forward until it finally hung down with its whole weight... and soon, the same would happen to me. Very soon we would both fall down and indifferently nuzzle a cold floor. But for some reason I had no fear of death, and waited patiently, caught up in a strange and surprising apathy for people, life, myself. I was already passing out when suddenly some person separated from the crowd and made his way towards us.

He was walking in our direction so confidently that despite my exhaustion and drowsiness, I instinctively moved away and put my arms forward to avoid a collision. But he stopped a half step away from us, and spoke with conviction, gesticulating vigorously and rather apprehensively, from time to time pointing at his throat and chest. His face seemed familiar. At last, through the noise of the tunnel, I managed to capture the sense of his words. We are dying.

"I am not scared," I said, or was it just a thought? You were totally motionless except for your heart. I could hardly feel your hand, cold as a dead person's hand, though your body was burning with fever. Plucking up my strength, I dug my elbow into your side.

"Damn, it's so cold here," you said, regaining consciousness. "And who the hell are you?"

"Looks like pneumonia. Does it hurt here? And here?" the young man asked, poking your chest and ignoring your question. "Try to give a cough."

He rushed into our stuffy tunnel like fresh air. Peering into a thin face squeezed by thick temples of glasses, I could finally recognize him. It was the son of that woman with a round face—our first mother, according to the list.

"You need to go to hospital, and you'd better hurry up," he concluded imperturbably.

"No, we don't need to," you reacted instantly.

His face was indistinct and vague as if I looked at it through a rain-streaked window. For a moment, I completely lost sight of him.

"Yes, you do, or else you're going to get into trouble," emptiness answered, turning into a human again.

"I don't care," your embittered voice croaked.

One way or the other the young man was likely to be the winner of the dispute, for it is not so difficult to win over two dying beggars, but at that moment Compass Legs unexpectedly arrived.

"What the fuck do you want?" he asked toughly, screwing up his face into an aggressive mask. "Come on; get out of here, smarty pants."

"They really need help, or else they'll get into mischief," the young man whom he called smarty pants protested.

"I said get the fuck out of my place!" was the rude response.

"Don't you have a bit of mercy for them?"

Compass Legs shrugged his sloping shoulders blankly and without further ado pushed the guy out of the tunnel. It became clear that there was no way out, or so it seemed to me. I don't remember how long we stood in the dark, outside our own minds, at the extremity and appendix of the world. It seemed like death would never come.

Despite frosty weather, the young man, whose name was Yuriy, was waiting for us outside the tunnel. As soon as we came into view, he grabbed us and helped us get home to the attic. He had brought some medication from the hospital where he worked as a doctor.

"What is it?" you asked apathetically at the sight of a syringe in his hand.

"It is no big deal," he replied with a slight smile. "It will feel like a mosquito bite."

"Are we going to die?" I asked quietly.

"Sometime you definitely will," Yura[23] responded reasonably and shrugged, "but not now, certainly not!"

He stayed with us through the entire night and left to go to work the following morning. One injection of medicine was not enough to cure us, and he kept coming every evening, bringing food and staying with us for long hours; a little later, he provided warm clothes and an old, thick blanket.

Every person has secret thoughts that he or she can only confide in a real friend or a soul mate; however, those are particularly scant for people like us. So far, everyone coming into our life has never stayed in it long enough to see the consequences of his actions. Will Yura feel a strong desire to remain our friend? Actually, it doesn't matter! All that mattered now was the fact that, for the first time in my life, I wanted to unburden my soul to someone. I was in such a rush to tell him *everything* that words literally jumped out of my mouth, escaped from my heart. Yura listened very attentively, not judging and not feeling sorry for us, just nodding from time to time, with a scarcely noticeable, ingenuous smile appearing on his lips from time to time.

In spite of the thin, slightly aquiline nose giving his oval face a characteristic hard look, he always emitted softness and warmth. He spoke just like everybody else, and at the same time in a way different from the others. He used to say, for instance, "smiley" instead of "smile", "trouble" instead of "grief", "pity" instead of "misery", "angel" instead of "dear" - those were seemingly ordinary words but they evoked positive and reassuring emotions and corresponding

---

23   Short name of *Yuriy*.

sentiments. We found out that outside the tunnel there was a great, amazing world where magic and miracles await everyone; the world where happiness can be endless and people capable of doing good things are not weaker than those who lust after power and authority, where only giving can actually make you richer. He believed in his words with all his heart, and it made me hold my breath in order not to scare away or destroy this *wonderful world of fairy tales*. And he kept on and kept on speaking and I felt very grateful to him for having made me see the true face of mankind, or his version of this true face.

One day he brought a friend with him. I felt awkward because we were going to see a stranger and didn't know how to act. Instinctively, I reached out for a blanket like someone or other reaches out for a towel after taking a shower.

"We brought some treats for you," Yura kindly cooed. "I believe you don't have lots of visitors today."

"I believe today is not a visiting day," I retorted, smiling, "unless you have an appointment."

"Of course we have." He was amazed by our diffidence. "My colleague and I have compelling reasons."

"It is a bad case, I see. However, my colleague," I pointed at you, "and I are deeply interested in it." I cheerfully winked at you. "So, what have you got?"

Yura lowered his gaze to the ground and answered:

"A kind of gingerbready gift for high-muck-a-muck's obedience and good behavior."

"Oh, so you're trying to bribe the official?" I could hardly help but burst out laughing.

"No, no, not at all. It's the samples."

"So why didn't you put them in a container?" you asked with genuine reproach.

After that question all of us fell about laughing.

"All right, let's go and prepare some reagents for clinical tests," I offered you.

"You mean some tea?" you asked with astonishment.

"No, tea is totally out of fashion now." I was genuinely amazed that anyone would dare to call things by their *improper* names. "In respectable houses, especially in white ones, they offer only reagents."

Awkwardness that had been brought about by the stranger's visit vanished like a mist. We all sat down at the "dining" table made from a set of empty buckets with a sheet of plywood on the top – our guests had providently brought cups and spoons with them – and had tea with gingerbread, talking and joking. Although, if the truth be told, the conversation was mostly led by Yura and his friend, a person with no name, no profession, no plans for the future and no face, as he described himself. In reality, he appeared to be a writer who hadn't published a single book. This strange man sank deep into my heart at once. He looked at everybody with fatherly feeling but at the same time estranged eyes. For the first time I saw a mix of childishness and senility in human eyes, nearly alien eyes. He told us mostly the same things as Yury did, but in absolutely different, simplified ways, reducing them to statements such as that one should always stay in one's own self, appreciate both bad and good things and take one's life easy as if it were a pleasantry. His thoughts poured out of him freely like water from a cloud, without any doubts or barriers.

"And what are your books about?" you interrupted him inappropriately.

"What they are not about, that is the question," the writer answered calmly and simply, and then suddenly added: "They *don't* narrate about delusions – that people with unusual or forbidding looks should be treated as if they were not human beings; that life finds its sense only in the midst of great suffering and tribulation; that it is difficult to smile to people who hate or despise you; that people's desires are primitive and life is complicated; that writing a book is equal to lounging; that being human is rather easy but seems to be quite superfluous to the average person. Perhaps my books are about worthwhile things *that don't seem to exist but are encountered every day."*

His speech was straightforward and decisive as if he took his last chance to speak out before his death. And while he shared his thoughts, I couldn't stop wondering why he took an interest in two conjoined girls rejected by everybody else and mostly unnoticed even in the most crowded places? However, that moment convinced me that our life – mine and yours – consists of trivial events and ludicrous losses; and if some writer decided to write a book about us, he would be absolutely puzzled as to where to begin and especially how to continue. Why did he come? The answer always hovered nearby, but I didn't dare grasp it.

"Why did you stop writing?" I inquired instead.

"I don't want to," he smiled gently. "I changed my mind."

"But there must be a reason."

"There is always a reason. I've been asked not to write, so I don't write."

"Just like that!" you couldn't help but wonder. "You stopped just because you were asked?"

"If someone, for whatever reason, doesn't want me to be a writer, well, probably I shouldn't write. I always try to respect what I'm requested to do," he answered calmly and confidently. "The main thing is to do no harm to others."

"He's such a nice guy!" Yura put in a word. "He is a yes-man. By the way, I asked him to come here with me, and, as you can see, he said yes and came."

"Life is very simple," the writer went on, explaining such wonderful and formerly inexplicable things. "The more you help someone, the more you get in return. I advise you to try, and then you'll see yourselves as you are and the world as it…"

"Nobody has ever helped us!" we exclaimed unanimously. "So why should we help anyone?"

"Are you sure about that? Maybe you just spare yourself the effort to notice?"

And at that moment my eyes met Yura's. Sure, I had been convincing myself that I was unworthy for so long that I ceased to recognize other people's help. Furthermore, because life had robbed us of luck and justice so casually, the number of our perpetual debtors owing us happiness had been growing every day.

"Yes, that's just how it goes," following our gaze, the writer continued, "no miracle; you change your point of view in the blink of an eye."

Still, I was reluctant to give up and tried to find some argument, just for spite's sake. For so many years we had been cultivating resentment towards the whole world that throwing it away now seemed not only impossible but fatal. We could only exchange it for something valid and reliable.

"It is hard to be fond of those who hate you," I expressed our common opinion.

"Are you sure they hate you?"

"You should've seen their faces!" you blurted out.

"Their faces are a reflection of yours. Try smiling in a mirror and it will smile in return. But someone has to be the first, so why don't you be the first?"

He said it with such a sincere smile that we involuntarily started smiling back.

"I dare say, my fellow, you are right; it really works," Yura said and started pulling funny faces, making us laugh until we cried.

Yeah, he was right, perfectly right. I always thought that people hate us for our dissimilarity, while in fact – only now I start to realize – they don't really care about us; everything we do in life is by our own and of our own free will and choice. We played *les misérables* hoping to squeeze out of people as much pity and money as possible, or, on the contrary, pretended to be like everybody else, hiding our differences behind our blanket, while all the while life had so much more to offer us. All our life had been filled with lies, deceit, play, dodging, trying to justify all our wrongdoings by believing in a regrettable necessity. Without meaning it, we chose isolation and somewhere halfway to this day, we killed the real us, leaving the entire world in a state of shock and fear. In other words, it appears that allowing grief and indignation to control our life, we merged with the crowd, as we have always dreamt it to be… but despite this, we are dissatisfied.

What is so special about an extraordinary person? An extraordinary person helps humans to understand that every person is extraordinary. Well, the writer made our entire life change, turning everything back to front but mysteriously allotting it its normal places. He came not because he wanted something from us – one can't get something from nothing – and not because Yury had asked him, but because we needed someone to lean on – a person with an amazing gift, that of turning every disadvantage into an advantage. From the very beginning, all our conversations resembled battles where he was the "subject of testing" (or the subject to test), of firmness, of certain convictions. He didn't try to disprove anything for any purpose, but somehow, everything turned out to be disproved in the end.

"We want to be like everybody else," I started, as usual.

"What do you need it for?"

He answered my question with a new question. Well, it did not actually bewilder me.

"In order not to stand out from others," I explained patiently.

He didn't even stir an eyelid.

"The fact of standing out and distinguishing yourself means that the person is unique."

I must honestly admit that he infuriated me and so I always kept on arguing. But the more I contemplated my sufferings, the more I suffered, and still didn't stop contemplating. Our conversations with him went something like this:

"What can be worse than being castaways? No one needs us."

"But you have each other; not everyone can boast of this privilege."

"We can never be each of us separately," you hissed with poorly hidden malice.

"On the other hand," the corners of his lips curled slightly upward, "you never know loneliness."

"We don't want to stand in the tunnel and seek charity; it is humiliating," we said unanimously.

"Everybody asks for something: help, friendship or blessing. Why not beg if someone is ready to donate to the needy? After all, the pleasure of giving is so much greater than receiving," he concluded. "The earlier you understand it, the sooner you will find happiness and make the world happy."

That evening, when he left, turning his back on us, I kept on seeing his smile for a long time afterwards – the smile of a child on an old man's lips.

* * *

Do you know what I'm thinking about? Is everything you perceive true, what you witness, the truth for everyone else? What if memories are just figments of one's imagination? You are still silent, aren't you?

I was awakened by a deafening silence, so profound that it seemed to have its own essence. A strange feeling dominated me, its strangeness familiar: a deep loneliness, and simultaneously the necessity to feel such loneliness. What am I so worried about? It is a beautiful, snowy winter day; a little New Year tree adorns one of the attic corners. Today is the last day of the year which is coming to an end, things are looking up. For the first time in our life we will have a real holiday, just like everybody else. Yura is coming soon to help us decorate our first New Year tree. I am so happy that I wouldn't even be afraid to die. I have only read it in books, but now I know how it really feels.

I heard the sound of footsteps on a concrete staircase...

You slept so peacefully and quietly that I didn't dare to awaken you. You're going to wake up by yourself, I decided. The footsteps ended and a long wiggling shadow appeared in the doorway of the attic. This is not Yura. The expectation lasts forever. Meanwhile, the silhouette determinedly looked around and quickly moved to us. I was enormously overwhelmed with fear and curiosity. The shadow came nearer, entering a better-lit area. Mixed feelings filled me – disappointment, annoyance, fear, hatred, helplessness – when I recognized Compass Legs's face. I always knew that he would come... and that very instant you opened your eyes.

"Peekaboo!" he hemmed. "Have you been waiting for me?"

"Yeah, right, all our thoughts were about you," you answered impudently.

"Well, perfectly well. And now, pick your asses up," he ordered brusquely, sending abundant spit onto the floor, "and march to work."

Not letting us come round, he shook us out of the blanket and towed us behind him to the exit.

"Don't touch her! She's feeling unwell," I begged for mercy. Perhaps we could put everything right between us and him, come to terms by mutual agreement, but...

"Fuck off, asshole! I'm not going anywhere!" you shrieked aloud. With rage, you thrust your nails into his neck.

Not expecting to encounter such a reaction, he was taken aback and got confused for an instant. Well, those magical instants are worth gold for a director, whoever he may be, and also for the public, who we truly are. Nonetheless, no moment lasts forever. Quite predictably, after regaining self-possession, Compass Legs slapped you in the face with all his might.

Absolute hatred permeated every fiber of my soul, and it seemed like someone else, not me, whipped out the screwdriver from your pocket. What was *that person* motivated by? Was it fear or loathing I harbored for that man? Is it possible to explain and justify everything with fear and loathing? Maybe explain, but not justify. It's too late now to say sorry. A screwdriver is already in my hands. Killing someone is so easy and, along with that, so revolting! At a loss, I pause for a fraction of a second or less, but alas, the difference between losers and winners is often thinner than a hair, and Compass Legs doesn't hesitate and acts at lightning-speed. He jerks the screwdriver out of my hand and lifts it above his head.

You know, Hope, I've got used to the feeling that death is always somewhere near, but who is going to be the first – you or me?

I close my eyes... hear a bump from inside and then nothing unexpected, just a screwdriver sticking out of your chest in the place where a heart should be. I feel strange relief, strange surprise: there is no pain, no fear, and no remorse. You're slowly going down: first your knees bend and only then you slump sideways, tugging at my sleeve and my hip.

"It is all her freaking fault, not mine. And you," Compass Legs grumbles apprehensively, pointing his finger at me, "you'd better not open your mouth, or else you'll follow your sister in a moment." And he vanishes into the dark as if that element were his life-companion.

I try to get up and look at you. You don't move, and, apparently, don't even breathe. I call your name, try to slap you in the face, and shout like an insane person so that everybody can hear: "It was me who provoked fate, attacking Compass Legs on purpose. For all my life I've been dreaming of getting rid of you, of my ballast, of escaping from the prison of our bodies." And now, when you are dying, I have the long-desired power to speak and act for both of us, live up to the hilt, but at the same time I can do nothing. If you don't live for me, I will die because of you. It is never going to end. Never! I am doomed to live with you forever and you are going to live and suffer with me. I will drag us to the staircase; don't you dare die on me. Don't you dare!"

I grasped your elbow and, thrusting my feet against the floor, tried to pull us up to the door. Like a worm in the sun,

I coiled next to your body, striving to move forward at least a little bit, but in vain. Summoning the last remnants of my strength, I jerked you by the hand with all the might I had, but you seemed to be glued to the floor. You're so heavy, Hope, so fucking heavy! Realizing my weakness, I yelled even harder, as hard as our mother must have yelled coughing us out into this world, putting into that yell everything I have ever experienced in my life: hatred, love, despair and hope. And then... How long did we lie on the floor?

When I regained consciousness, feeling deep pain in my cheek, I saw a thin face hovering in front of me. It was Yura's, and he was giving me another slap in the face. This morning everyone seemed to be conspiring to beat us without permission.

"Do you hear me?" he shouts.

Yes, I hear his voice, but somewhere far away from here. He applies his sweater to your chest, feels your pulse.

"What happened?"

"It was me..." I pause, not able to continue. Yura frowns, but abstains from further inquiries. "Is she dead?"

"No, she's still breathing," he answers. "It is a miracle that she is still alive. I called an ambulance; they are going to be here in a minute."

"It's my fault," I say almost inaudibly. "I always wanted to live without her."

"Keep quiet, you'll tell *everything* later," he smiles understandingly. "Now you're wasting her strength."

And he took me by the hand and kept holding it in the ambulance car and in the hospital.

They're rolling us somewhere on the gurney. There is a narrow, endless corridor, shabby walls and a row of lamps floating along the ceiling. You might probably know, this hospital corridor reminds me of human life – no one can see where it ends, no one can remember where it begins, no one can be told what it is. In the operating theater doctors are hanging over us like flat, white shadows, dividing us with a screen, so that I can no longer see you with my eyes. I know as soon as I fall asleep I will never wake up again. I fight to keep my eyes wide open with all the feeble strength that remains in us, seeking to stay in this world a little longer, but the desire to sleep is so excessive and so abnormal.

I'm slowly waking up after anesthesia. A small hospital room with a clean window; it is snowing outside. I am very happy to see the light of the day.

"Do you feel nauseous?" a hospital attendant asks.

I shake my head and then ask him faintly, "Is my sister okay?"

"Everything is all right," a familiar voice says, and Yura appears before the window.

"I'll see about telling her everything, so please leave us alone," he addresses the hospital attendant who places his palms one against the other, in front of his chest, takes a deep breath and immediately goes out.

"Your sister... she is recovering after the surgery. The screwdriver pierced her lung, and she lost a lot of blood. But don't worry, her heart was not affected... for it is located on the right side of her body," he speaks as if to himself.

I nod silently in response. Where did all those nice, sweet words, the integral part of his repertoire, go? He is so serious – frighteningly serious!

"I have *good* news for you," he starts almost whispering. "I found a doctor who is capable of performing separation surgery. A big dream of yours is coming true, finally. But I don't think we should wake Hope up. She needs a rest; you will tell her later."

I stare at him, dumbfounded with shock, deafened by internal roaring. Can it be that we shall be hived off, split up in two halves, so that each one will become an independent person? I am so scared, Hope. Now when I am so close to the goal, I am so terribly scared!

"You are so cold! You must be absolutely freezing. Let me cover you," Yura says and puts a blanket over us. His eyes are red; I think he's just tired. Only now do I understand that for the first time in my life I am watching him in a white robe, his white robe.

"You look so tired, you need to rest and recover because you are doing too much," I tell him, but he doesn't move. "Hey, you must be going. See you tomorrow."

"Yeah, right, see you," he says, clumsily backing to the door. "Oh, no, wait a minute."

He takes a piece of paper out of his pocket and comes up to our bed.

"Here, it dropped out of your pocket. I'll put it on the bedside table."

Then he leaves us alone for the evening.

Shortly after, I reach out to the bedside table and take the drawing. Dampness and time have made it worn, blurred, faded, reminding me of a smudgy blot. No one can tell now how many people it depicts and whether they are beautiful or ugly... but I think everything's beautiful that is done through the human heart and soul, that makes our inner world visible, that gives us a chance to look at ourselves from the outside in – everything is beautiful, even us. But this life isn't endless; we need to hurry, to have the time to do great things, to put the most important things into words, too. How much I love you, Hope! I am so sorry I didn't tell you this before. I will surely do so, as soon as you wake up... so that I can, *at last*, fall asleep.

But before that I need to tell you so many things. Very soon, there will be no "us". There will only be "you" and "me", separately, and nevertheless, we will never stop being one whole. You in Me and Me in You. *My God, it's so cold. You look happy while asleep and I can't stop thinking about how cold I am. Why is it so chilly here? I just can't get warm like in the hospital when they plunged us into icy water...*

I shiver all over with fear and shame, but I can neither leave, nor go inside; my feet are groaning and buzzing as if nailed to the hospital floor. For many hours I've been standing behind the door and listening eagerly, catching every word spilled from her lips. Yura is sitting on a near window sill, his face turned away, and only the reflection in the window reveals that he is crying – crying because of his inability to do anything. Today he lied for the first time in his life, for he couldn't summon the courage to tell the truth: Hope is already gone, and Faith will be the last to die. But so far... Yura has asked me to stay with Faith until she falls asleep... forever. And I can't say no.

Eventually, the voice behind the door falls silent, having finished the retelling of the story already told. I go inside and close the door behind me.

"You're in time," Faith says to me.

I take out an orange and hand it to her, wishing her a happy new year.

"Thank you," she answers politely and puts the orange on the bedside table. "We will eat it together when Hope wakes up."

I nod and give a silly smile.

"You were right, it is always the right time to do the right thing, not once in a lifetime, but always before it's too late," she says, peering into the blackness outside the window. "You

know what is amusing? All I did before was try to shorten our lives, but now the only thing I think about is how to make them longer. There is so much to live for: life is amazing and full of miracles; too bad I didn't notice it before, and good that I understand it a little better now. Maybe you should write about it, to remind everyone."

And, turning her face to me, she declares:

"Please, tell them my story, will you? Don't say no; I'm asking you. I believe in you like you believed in me once. Help people to find hope and never lose faith, so that they can see how wonderful life is."

For now I don't really understand why I came to them – not because I needed help – actually, the right to help someone is something you need to deserve – but did I need their help? Her request is a chance for me to start writing again. I will achieve so much later.

"We will tell you everything as it was. Perhaps, Hope won't mind. I'm going to ask her when she wakes up."

Now it's the right time to do the right thing, to become the person I always wanted to be.

"I believe that she will agree," she adds. "So, will you write?"

"I will," I answer.

This is what I will have to live with. Not just live, but also bring myself to the judgment of my readers, probably, no less severe than myself. My God, it's really so cold here.

For several years I have been collecting the records from the heroes of this book for this book. But I could not find everyone, and not everyone agreed to talk to me; I had to figure out many facts.

This novel is in no way a confession about how hard it is and how long it takes to write a book and how little truth remains in the end, nor is it a book of complaints. It is a chance to be sincere with myself. Most of all, it's a chance to be sincere with you; not everybody is that happy.

For more than fifteen years I have been hesitating. Should I publish this story? I kept writing and rewriting, forgetting and finding my way back, only to forget again. But now, I believe the right time has come. I hope this book is for you.

Contents

Forefathers' Eve

by Adam Mickiewicz

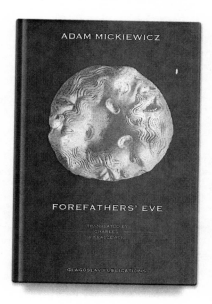

Forefathers' Eve [Dziady] is a four-part dramatic work begun circa 1820 and completed in 1832 – with Part I published only after the poet's death, in 1860. The drama's title refers to *Dziady*, an ancient Slavic and Lithuanian feast commemorating the dead. This is the grand work of Polish literature, and it is one that elevates Mickiewicz to a position among the "great Europeans" such as Dante and Goethe.

With its Christian background of the Communion of the Saints, revenant spirits, and the interpenetration of the worlds of time and eternity, *Forefathers' Eve* speaks to men and women of all times and places. While it is a truly Polish work – Polish actors covet the role of Gustaw/Konrad in the same way that Anglophone actors covet that of Hamlet – it is one of the most universal works of literature written during the nineteenth century. It has been compared to Goethe's Faust – and rightfully so…

Buy it > www.glagoslav.com

Leo Tolstoy – Flight from Paradise

by Pavel Basinsky

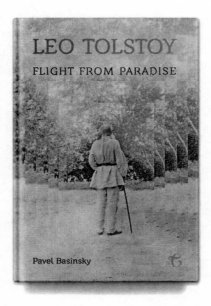

Over a hundred years ago, something truly outrageous occurred at Yasnaya Polyana. Count Leo Tolstoy, a famous author aged eighty-two at the time, took off, destination unknown. Since then, the circumstances surrounding the writer's whereabouts during his final days and his eventual death have given rise to many myths and legends. In this book, popular Russian writer and reporter Pavel Basinsky delves into the archives and presents his interpretation of the situation prior to Leo Tolstoy's mysterious disappearance. Basinsky follows Leo Tolstoy throughout his life, right up to his final moments. Reconstructing the story from historical documents, he creates a visionary account of the events that led to the Tolstoys' family drama.

Flight from Paradise will be of particular interest to international researchers studying Leo Tolstoy's life and works, and is highly recommended to a broader audience worldwide.

Buy it > www.glagoslav.com

Dear Reader,

Thank you for purchasing this book.

We at Glagoslav Publications are glad to welcome you, and hope that you find our books to be a source of knowledge and inspiration. We want to show the beauty and depth of the Slavic region to everyone looking to expand their horizon and learn something new about different cultures and different people, and we believe that with this book we have managed to do just that.

Now that you've gotten to know us, we want to get to know you. We value communication with our readers and want to hear from you! We offer several options:

– Join our Book Club on Goodreads, Library Thing and Shelfari, and receive special offers and information about our giveaways;

– Share your opinion about our books on Amazon, Barnes & Noble, Waterstones and other bookstores;

– Join us on Facebook and Twitter for updates on our publications and news about our authors;

– Visit our site www.glagoslav.com to check out our Catalogue and subscribe to our Newsletter.

Glagoslav Publications is getting ready to release a new collection and planning some interesting surprises — stay with us to find out more!

Glagoslav Publications
Office 36, 88-90 Hatton Garden
EC1N 8PN London, UK
Tel: + 44 (0) 20 32 86 99 82
Email: contact@glagoslav.com

Glagoslav Publications Catalogue

- The Time of Women by Elena Chizhova
- Sin by Zakhar Prilepin
- Hardly Ever Otherwise by Maria Matios
- Khatyn by Ales Adamovich
- Christened with Crosses by Eduard Kochergin
- The Vital Needs of the Dead by Igor Sakhnovsky
- A Poet and Bin Laden by Hamid Ismailov
- Kobzar by Taras Shevchenko
- White Shanghai by Elvira Baryakina
- The Stone Bridge by Alexander Terekhov
- King Stakh's Wild Hunt by Uladzimir Karatkevich
- Depeche Mode by Serhii Zhadan
- Herstories, An Anthology of New Ukrainian Women Prose Writers
- The Battle of the Sexes Russian Style by Nadezhda Ptushkina
- A Book Without Photographs by Sergey Shargunov
- Sankya by Zakhar Prilepin
- Wolf Messing by Tatiana Lungin
- Good Stalin by Victor Erofeyev
- Solar Plexus by Rustam Ibragimbekov
- Don't Call me a Victim! by Dina Yafasova
- A History of Belarus by Lubov Bazan
- Children's Fashion of the Russian Empire by Alexander Vasiliev
- Boris Yeltsin - The Decade that Shook the World by Boris Minaev
- A Man Of Change - A study of the political life of Boris Yeltsin
- Gnedich by Maria Rybakova
- Marina Tsvetaeva - The Essential Poetry
- Multiple Personalities by Tatyana Shcherbina
- The Investigator by Margarita Khemlin
- Leo Tolstoy – Flight from paradise by Pavel Basinsky
- Moscow in the 1930 by Natalia Gromova
- Prisoner by Anna Nemzer
- Alpine Ballad by Vasil Bykau
- The Complete Correspondence of Hryhory
- The Tale of Aypi by Ak Welsapar
- Selected Poems by Lydia Grigorieva
- The Fantastic Worlds of Yuri Vynnychuk
- The Garden of Divine Songs and Collected Poetry of Hryhory Skovoroda
- Adventures in the Slavic Kitchen: A Book of Essays with Recipes
- Forefathers' Eve by Adam Mickiewicz
- Seven Signs of the Lion by Michael M. Naydan

More coming soon...

CPSIA information can be obtained
at www.ICGtesting.com
Printed in the USA
LVOW12s1826300317
529062LV00004B/645/P